I found the book interesting, meaty, well written. A treasure of a book, thoughtful and analytical. In our fast-paced and hectic world, we can often miss what it really means to love God. The key is balance, coming to Him with our whole selves.

—Nancie Carmichael
author and founding co-publisher of *Virtue* magazine

Judith Hougen's clear, captivating writing rings true and awakens our desires and hopes to discover our authentic selves in God. She graciously encourages readers to explore the richness of contemplative practices which invite God's transforming presence and love. This is a book for anyone who seeks to be and become fully God's, fully alive.

—Jeannette A. Bakke
author of *Holy Invitations: Exploring Spiritual Direction*
Faculty Associate, Bethel Theological Seminary

Easy to read and comprehend, yet intellectually substantial. I loved Judy's book and couldn't recommend it more highly. Indeed, it met me at a time when I needed to be reminded that the gospel is true—that this "Good News" we preach really is the best news of all!

—Rev. David W. Johnson
Senior Pastor at Church of the Open Door, Maple Grove, Minn.
author of *The Subtle Power of Spiritual Abuse* and
Joy Comes in the Mourning

Transformed *into* Fire

Transformed *into* Fire

An Invitation
to Life in
the True Self

JUDITH HOUGEN

Kregel
Publications

Transformed into Fire: An Invitation to Life in the True Self

© 2002 by Judith Hougen

Published by Kregel Publications, a division of Kregel, Inc., P.O. Box 2607, Grand Rapids, MI 49501. For more information about Kregel Publications, visit our Web site: www.kregel.com.

Cover design: John M. Lucas

Library of Congress Cataloging-in-Publication Data
Hougen, Judith.
    Transformed into fire: an invitation to life in the true self / by Judith Hougen.
        p. cm.
Includes bibliographical references.
    1. Christian Life. I. Title.
BV4501.3 .H68   2002   248.4—dc21   2002009872

ISBN 0-8254-2890-4

Printed in the United States of America

02 03 04 05 06 / 5 4 3 2 1

To all of the students
who have allowed me to walk alongside them
in their journeys.
Your search for life helped forge these words.

For my Savior Jesus Christ—
Master, Lover, Teacher, Friend—
you are all the world to me.

CONTENTS

PREFACE

*L*ast spring, when I taught a class on Christianity and writing, I received the following words from Corinne, a beautiful young woman who is one of my writing majors:

> I do not think that God cares that every time it rains, warmth spreads over me and brings brightness to my face. He really doesn't care that I love the stars or that I collect bronzed leaves in my notebook each fall. He is sovereign, looking down on me with expressionless eyes. He is waiting for the time when I will be more "focused" and "together," completely absorbed in Christian service. Preferably in the place I least desire—Siberia or Russia, where I will never be warm again and will eat cold, gray mush every day. If you ask me whether I believe God loves me unconditionally, I would proclaim most emphatically, "YES!" But do I truly believe that? I don't. I know I'm wrong, but I can't believe otherwise; my cry is that he helps my unbelief.

Does this sound anything like your life? If so, you're not alone.

As a fellow sojourner, I've been in the place that Corinne writes about—desiring to love God with my whole being, doubting the intensity of God's love for me, praying through my own periods of unbelief. Within all of us lives a deep hunger to love God with our whole self, yet we seem to have few guides to authentically assist us in this journey.

The guides that gather into these pages come from my evangelical circle as well as from elsewhere within the Christian tradition. While I might have theological differences with some of these authors, many of their reflections have enlivened my journey. I am grateful for the truths they have to speak. A few of their ideas—and specifically practices such as *lectio divina* and centering prayer—may seem foreign. I invite you to make such places points of prayer.

My hope in writing is that you'll discover that the Christian life is sweeter than anyone has ever told you and that God is more tender, more gracious and intimate than your mind can ever conceive.

I pray that the Lord will meet you and transform you within these words.

ACKNOWLEDGMENTS

While I spent many days alone, tapping out these words, this book is, in reality, a product of community. My gratitude goes to all who lent valuable support to this project: Sara Anderson, Mary Ellen Ashcroft, Jan Bros, Eric Johnson, and Peggy Lang. Thanks also to all who prayed this book into existence, in particular my prayer team: Sara, Becki, Leah, Doug and Peggy, Matt and Sarah, John and Lisa, Viv and Larry, Geri, Karen, Heather, Felicia. There were many moments when I knew I was buoyed on the prayers of my community.

I also thank all the folks who shared their journeys with me and put flesh on many of these ideas. Your thirst for God in hard places points to the magnificence of grace. I'm honored to include your thoughts and stories.

Finally, special gratitude is due to two people in particular: Heather Walker, my friend and colleague, read and critiqued every word of this manuscript—and brought dinner on many summer nights as I completed this project. Similarly, Scott Bernstein pored over each chapter as it was completed and encouraged this project when it was nothing more than random ideas scattered on the table during lunch.

I have come that they may have life, and have it to the full.
—*Jesus (John 10:10)*

If anyone would come after me, he must deny himself and take up his cross daily and follow me. For whoever wants to save his life will lose it, but whoever loses his life for me will save it. What good is it for a man to gain the whole world, and yet lose or forfeit his very self?
—*Jesus (Luke 9:23–27)*

We only live, only suspire
Consumed by either fire or fire.
—*T. S. Eliot*

1

THE CALL TO COMMUNION

*Dear reader, there is nothing in this universe that is easier to
obtain than the enjoyment of Jesus Christ! Your Lord is more
present to you than you are to yourself! Furthermore, His
desire to give Himself to you is greater than your desire to
lay hold of Him.*

—Jeanne Guyon

I will sing of your love and justice;
to you, O LORD, I will sing praise.
I will be careful to lead a blameless life—
when will you come to me?

—David (Psalm 101:1–2)

Karen had been raised in a Christian home in the Midwest.*
Both of her parents were well educated and active in church
life. Karen—a typical church kid—grew up involved in youth

---

* Names and some details have been changed to protect the privacy of
those whose stories appear.

group and eventually attended the conservative Christian college where I teach. Despite Karen's religious background, however, struggle had always marked her spiritual life. In the two years that she spent at the college, that struggle still tore at her relationship with God. She was unable (or perhaps unwilling) to be vulnerable with God, to let him meet her deepest needs. Yes, Karen knew all *about* God, but her faith was based on performance rather than a relationship of the heart. She knew that God *should* be able to fill the empty place in her heart, but the path to that place seemed blocked.

At the end of her sophomore year, Karen met Matt, a man whose experience with God was similar to hers. Abandoning their faith, Karen and Matt attempted to meet each other's spiritual needs, conjuring human versions of unconditional love, acceptance, and grace. Eventually, they became involved sexually, and she dropped out of school. When asked about this relationship, which she knew to be a product of sin, Karen said, "If I have to choose between God and Matt, I'll choose Matt."

Angie also hungered for a deeper connection with God. Pretty and full of life, she was raised in a godly family with many relatives who dedicated their lives to ministry work. But some emotional and spiritual abuse she suffered as a child hung over her heart. Sitting on my living room couch for a time of prayer, we shared our journeys. To do a quick diagnosis of how she viewed God, I said to her, "Imagine that Jesus is coming into this room right now. He's walking in the door. He's looking around the room, and he sees you. He's approaching, and now he's sitting down right next to you. What do you think he wants to say to you?" At these words, Angie visibly tensed, almost curling into a ball. She clearly thought of Jesus as some sort of enemy, yet she was preparing for international missions work. This woman was, in essence, planning on traveling a few thousand miles to invite others into a life she herself was not experiencing, with a God who frightened her.

As crazy as this scenario sounds, it's far from unusual. Like Angie and Karen, my friend Doug desired a love for God that was rooted in more than cognitive understanding. He felt he was missing out on something, and the church he attended at that time—a place that emphasized the intellect—seemed impotent to help him. Doug felt spiritually deficient because he seldom sensed the presence of God in his study and worship. He compensated by plunging into various ministries in which he was quite visible. Still desperate to taste more, Doug began attending an extremist charismatic church, in hopes of attaining a deeper connection to God. He believed a spiritually dynamic setting might provide the right experience and provoke the desired response in his heart. In time, he became focused on demonstrative things—such as speaking in tongues—as a way to prove to himself that he really was a complete believer whom God noticed and loved.

There's something very wrong in these stories. But because the realities they represent are typical within our faith communities, we dare not label them tragic. If we did, we'd have to admit that the Christian church is daily, hourly, mired in tragedy. We would have to admit that Rome is burning, and we're sitting around singing campfire songs.

Like all of us, the people in these stories are on a search, a search for love, tenderness, and intimacy where their deepest needs, the hungers of their hearts, will be met. Karen, Angie, and Doug attempted to follow the map of faith that they were handed. And, as is true for many of us, the journey was marred by disappointment, frustration, and a preoccupation with pursuits that missed the mark. Each of them understood the Bible. Each was exposed to sound, orthodox teaching on Christianity. So, what went wrong? Did God create within us a longing for a destination he never intended for us to reach? Why do we so often miss him in the search, and how do we even begin the journey?

Many churched people have a spiritual life that's like a car, sputtering down the highway, coughing and jerking, red engine lights flashing. The driver's solution is to beat a fist on the dashboard until the warning lights quit flashing. He or she motors on, believing that eliminating the warning signs is the same as fixing the problem.[1]

This is how most Christians are taught to treat the spiritual predicaments in which they find themselves. When warning lights flash in their relationship with God, try harder, read the Bible more, pound on the spiritual dashboard until the warnings cease. But it's never enough, and nothing permanently changes. Something is wrong in the engine—the machinery of faith, the inner workings, are seriously impaired. We need to stop, pull over, and open the hood. But we're afraid—afraid of God and of ourselves. And afraid, perhaps, that what's broken is beyond repair.

Across America all kinds of people—conservatives, liberals, young, old, strutting in suits, lounging in jeans—enter and exit churches every week. They carry Bibles, commentaries, notebooks. The faithful come and go, pondering Sunday sermons or Sunday dinner. Yet, if all these people were polled, the vast majority would likely agree with this statement: I *know* that God loves me, but I rarely or never *experience* his love.

Within such a profession, something is seriously amiss. A terrible chasm yawns between knowing and experiencing, fact and faith, ideas and action. In short, there's a disconnection between the head and the heart.

Head is a term for intellect, the place where facts and ideas are received and stored. We learn, for instance, that the Declaration of Independence was signed in 1776. It's a fact and our head stores it. *Heart* engages with experience—sensory impressions and emotion. The heart represents the deep self that is present to and responds to physical and emotional stimuli. We might attend an Independence Day parade and the experience of that—the colors, sounds, smells—is received in the heart. Thus the abstract historical event and our experience of the parade are not received in the same way.

Scripture, too, recognizes the distinction between knowing with the head and knowing with the heart. Through the prophet Jeremiah, God says, "I will put my law in their minds and write it on their hearts" (31:33). In the Psalms, God "searches minds and hearts" (7:9), and David asks God to "examine my heart and my mind" (26:2). And when an expert in the law quizzed Jesus for the greatest commandment, he answered, "Love the Lord your God with all your heart and with all your soul and with all your mind" (Matt. 22:37). Together, the heart and head constitute the self whom we are and the self who engages life on all levels. The preceding Scriptures reflect a desire to be immersed in God's law *completely,* to search and be searched *completely,* and to love God *completely. Head* and *heart* are a way to talk about our complete selves.

Unfortunately, forces both within and around us have created a disconnection between the head and the heart. Our experiential knowledge of God is usually so barren, so bereft of the Master's touch, that we dismiss it as unnecessary, saying that cognitive knowledge of God's presence is all we need. Or we claim that knowing God in our actual living, our experiences, is something lesser that only unbalanced believers chase after.

Yet within us all is a craving of the spirit, a yearning to abide in God's heart, a longing for grace beyond theory. Have you desired it? Do you dare to admit it? We hunger to be overtaken by the fierce love of God that is spread across the pages of the Bible:

> Come, all you who are thirsty,
>   come to the waters;
> and you who have no money,
>   come, buy and eat!
> Come, buy wine and milk
>   without money and without cost.
> Why spend money on what is not bread,
>   and your labor on what does not satisfy?
> Listen, listen to me, and eat what is good,
>   and your soul will delight in the richest of fare.
> Give ear and come to me;
>   hear me, that your soul may live.
>
>   —Isaiah 55:1–3

This Scripture reveals a God who, at the banquet hall of his love, almost tears the doors from their hinges to create easier access for his beloved people. God serves the only feast that will ever satisfy, and yet he is not above imploring, even begging, those who have grown accustomed to their deprivation to come, feed, and be blessed.

The life lived in Jesus is not only a feast, it is a story of two lovers who desire, who experience, an ever-deepening intimacy. We were created to walk through our brief time on earth hand in hand with our Bridegroom. The Scriptures, the long love letter from our Beloved, speak of God's passionate, irrevocable affection for his creation. This passion is not romantic hyperbole or a poetic way of talking about faith. Rather, it is intended to be the norm for believers. Still, we seem to have largely missed such passion, wandering through our days as if it were beyond our reach.

But such passion constitutes a treasure, very real and very near, as close as your next breath. You may encounter that treasure by the opening of your whole self to God, by realizing you are the beloved, forever accepted, fully alive in a wondrous "yes" to the very life of God.

Whether or not we know it, we are all searching for the treasure. And if we do not find it in the Lover of our souls, we will seek it in far lesser places. We look for it in human relationships, success, substances. But all journeys to possess a deeply felt, rock-solid love and acceptance are ultimately the search for God.

But barriers impede the journey. The faith most of us have been handed is almost entirely cognitive, a relationship based on the ideas that we form about God or the ideas that we direct toward him. We have come to define *belief* as only intellectual decision and assent. Love, mercy, grace, sanctification—all are abstractions rather than living, daily realities, experiences that enflame the soul. If the heart enters into the spiritual equation, it slips through the back door—usually via the weekend retreat or the mountaintop worship experience. On occasion,

God's love is received in ways that embrace our hearts, and we sense we are beholding our Maker face-to-face. But such moments pass, and we have no map by which to retrace our steps to that place of intimacy and tenderness.

A change, a healing is needed. Our head and heart need to be in accord, both receiving the same truths. While our heads are verdant gardens, full of the knowledge of God, too often our hearts are deserts, dry and empty, crying, "I know nothing of him!"

Head and Heart: Finding Belief

When I was in the first grade, my teacher taught me that 2 + 2 = 4. Once my head—that is, my intellect—understood this rudimentary calculation, I believed it, accepted it, and stored it away as fact. The head can receive a great deal of truth without ever engaging the heart because there's a significant difference in how the head and the heart come to believe. The matter of 2 + 2 = 4 was settled as soon as my objective, logical understanding accepted it as reality. When the intellect engages with a fact, the fact is stored as truth, and belief results.

In contrast, the heart believes only what it experiences. The heart is hardly swayed by analytical ideas and logical conclusions. Cognitive fact has no place to lodge in the heart—its currency consists of the emotions and images of daily life. Thus, the heart, in order to become convinced of a truth, needs physical or psychological experience. If a friend gives me a hug or if I laugh during a funny movie, I receive a different internal impression than if I only cognitively know that my friend loves me or understand that the movie is reported to be humorous.

Senses and emotions process reality differently than does the intellect, and the result of that process leaves a unique psychic imprint. We're created to establish belief through two pathways—cognitive and experiential, that is, head and heart. And only when both pathways are engaged does belief become complete and actual.

A child named Alice, for example, is periodically told by her parents that she is loved very much. But the parents never demonstrate their love with hugs or special attention. As Alice grows, a dissonance arises. Her intellect says, "My parents love me; they told me so, and parents are supposed to love their children." But without actual experience—hugs and attention—to complete the idea of love, Alice has difficulty internalizing that reality. Soon Alice's parents question her disinterest in spending time with them or approaching them when she feels burdened. Alice's reluctance to draw near arises because her head accepted the idea behind the verbalized "I love yous," but her heart could not. Thus, Alice has difficulty relating to her parents as if she's truly loved because she has no tangible knowledge of their love.

Is this a thumbnail sketch of your spiritual life? It is for many Christians. You understand the doctrine of God's love, but you may not know how to receive and experience this love, secretly wondering if God even likes you. The lives of many Christians are an argument in which their heads tell them one thing while their hearts assert the opposite. The head and the heart are thus divided.

When I was sixteen my family moved to a small community in Wisconsin, where we lived in a housing development surrounded by farms. My aunt and uncle had given me a devotional book, *The Way* by E. Stanley Jones, and I would walk with book in hand to a quiet place near our house. A creek tumbled through a pasture, and I would sit on a ledge below a bridge and watch the sun rise high in the morning. It was a little patch of solace and beauty, and I wanted to go there with God. I wanted him to enjoy that setting with me, to speak through E. Stanley's archaic diction and to unfold his thoughts in my heart.

My romantic vision of meeting God in the pasture never lived up to my expectations. But an innocent goodness spurred that vision, and I remember that place as a symbol of my yearning for a heart relationship with God. I had a desire to know

God beyond ideas and doctrines. I wanted his story to be my story. So I did all the right things—Bible studies, youth group, Christian college. Still, even as I grew wealthier in knowledge, I felt impoverished inside. Something was missing—a sense of intimacy, a feeling of being at home with God.

I never constantly or deeply felt God's acceptance. I thought of myself as the rich young man to whom Jesus said, "One thing you lack." That lack became a steady hunger in my twenties, and while I could see the desired end, I had little clue how to get there. I understood the love of God conceptually, but except for an occasional kum-bah-yah experience around the campfire, I had no emotional or experiential knowledge of God. I finally came to a point in my spiritual journey where I said, "I don't want to learn anything more about God unless I can also experience that reality!" My life with Jesus was dry as sand, my prayers were perfunctory, my Bible study tasted like spiritual mind candy. There was no passion.

My spiritual journey at this point was not a quest to accumulate new information about God. I lacked no vital piece of truth; I needed the truths stored in my head to filter into my heart. I required not more information but deep response, not to feed the head but to ignite the heart.

The Great Divide

The focus on intellectual assent is not a modern phenomenon. In the sixteenth century, philosopher Rene Descartes penned his famous dictum, "I think therefore I am." The philosophical constructs that surrounded this phrase exalted intellectual self-awareness as the center of existence—to the detriment of life in Christ: "From the understanding that God had 'thought' them into existence, creating them in His image, Christians and Jews alike began with Descartes to try to think themselves into existence."[2] An imbalance resulted, weighing the value of the intellect much more heavily than other human faculties, even—as is true for so many today—above God.

Then during the Enlightenment in the 1700s, society became increasingly secularized, and exciting discoveries in science eclipsed God as the center of life and knowledge. The human mind, it seemed, was limitless and capable of analyzing and comprehending everything that was truly valuable.

The church gradually accommodated the mood of the general culture, creating a faith that revolved around intellectual and analytical pursuits of God. While many spiritual leaders taught that knowing God was *not* separate from experiencing God, nonetheless over the centuries, cognitive assent *replaced* heart response. An overemphasis on abstract truths of God crowded out transforming love.

Thus, in much of Christianity today, when it comes to experiencing God, the head is disconnected from the heart. And this schism between head and heart has produced a huge spiritual tension in Christendom. Of course, intellectual assent to the truths of God is essential, but it is incomplete. And while we need sound theological truth to build a strong faith foundation, intellectual truth is not all that we need. To heal the head/heart schism that too often characterizes our life with God, the distinction between communication and communion must first be understood.

Communication and Communion

Think about how you interact with the person whom you most love on this earth—what you say, how you say it. Contrast that with how you relate to a person who's lost in your neighborhood and asks you for directions. There is, of course, a qualitative difference between how we speak with some people versus others. We talk differently to our friends or loved ones than to the person who bags our groceries. The first scenario is characterized by communion, the other by communication. These are humanity's two primary ways of interacting.[3] Communication and communion are expressions of the head and the heart.

Communication is information received by the head—it is "logical, quantitative, and practical in its application."[4] Communication is necessary to trade ideas, to give commands, and to generally get things done. It focuses on tasks or delivers needed data. Communion, on the other hand, is information received by the heart—its purpose is not solely to deliver data but to touch us in a deep, personal way. Communion focuses on fostering relationships. The information expressed is not an end in itself but the means to creating a more intimate bond between the speaker and the listener.

We freely and accurately shift between communication and communion in our daily lives. A boss, for example, tells her assistant, "I need the Johnson report by one o'clock." The information transmitted is communication, meant to be received primarily by the intellect and acted on accordingly. But on his lunch break, the assistant gets a phone call from his closest friend, who says, "I just called to say how much our friendship means to me. Thanks for being there for me through the years." This information is not meant to be received as pure intellectual fact—that is, communication—but as communion. The friend's aim is not to enlighten the assistant with previously unknown information. Nor is the information needed to accomplish any particular task. The assistant understands that his friend's intent is to express a powerful truth that draws the friend to him and to forge a deeper relationship.

We have little trouble distinguishing between communication and communion in our everyday experiences. The majority of the time, we can readily identify the intention of both the speaker and the information and respond appropriately. The friend would be hurt were the assistant to react in a cold, intellectual way to a loving declaration, just as the boss would be surprised if the assistant hugged her after hearing her request for work to be done.

But our lives with God are another matter. Most Christians only know how to spiritually function on the communication level. In theory we probably acknowledge God as the tenderhearted friend, but in practice the God we open ourselves to is the boss who approaches with a list of duties.

The Heart of the Matter

My friend Barbara has been a part of church life from baby-hood on—from showing up for kindergarten Sunday school in her patent leather shoes, to baptism at age nine, to teen youth events. But when she reflects on her formative spiritual experiences, what she sees is a life of communication: "It amazes me because my church was big on the Bible, but what was modeled and taught was a collection of information about God. Your spiritual growth was measured by how much information you had about God. My idea of being a Christian was about what was in my head."

Without a relationship with God that combined communication and communion— head and heart—Barbara sought communion elsewhere. She entered into a relationship with a non-Christian boyfriend, whom she eventually married and later divorced. Barbara has since received healing and restoration and is today in a strong, balanced relationship with God. But she still thinks about what was missing in her early church experience: "I had a lot of solid Bible teaching. I knew how to go to church every week. But I don't remember ever thinking there was more to it than that until much later when my life became painful."

In the majority of churches, the Sunday service rarely strays from the communication path, which celebrates intellectual truth of God. Sunday mornings, by and large, cater to the head, chauffeuring the intellect around in a spiritual limousine while the heart holds out its thumb on the roadside.

As a child and a young adult, I sat through church services, absentmindedly fingering the wooden pew arm while the truth of God flew around the room. Utterly impassive, removed, I took in the clichéd, "God loves you. Jesus died for you," as if I'd just been handed a mathematical equation. For many, the concept of God's love remains just that—a concept, a cloud of Bible verses floating somewhere "out there." We are rarely drawn into God's embrace, the place where the communion we were created for fans into flame.

How many times in the last few months have you heard about the love of God through sermons, Bible study, or friends? Did that news ever once send an electric shiver down your spine? Did any of those experiences make you feel vulnerable and tender, as when you receive a dozen roses and a kiss from your beloved? Your knees needn't buckle every time you encounter the truth of your belovedness, but if they *never* do, then the balance between communion and communication is tragically tilted.

We were not created to possess ideas about God but to be possessed by him in the way a husband and wife possess each other through loving commitment and intimate attraction. God fashioned us for love, and all heaven holds its breath to see if we will love him back, waits for our inmost self to burn with passion in response to his pursuit. Put this book down for a moment and meditate on the spirit of our Beloved:

> The LORD your God is with you,
> he is mighty to save.
> He will take great delight in you,
> he will quiet you with his love,
> he will rejoice over you with singing.
> —Zephaniah 3:17

In silent awe and amazement, drink in the loving-kindness of God, the realization that you are so thoroughly treasured by your heart's one treasure. This is communion. Can the truth of God's delight in you slip into your emotions and experience, your deep self, not just your intellect? If not, you're far from alone.

From Codes to Communion

So many of us miss out on communion, because for so long it has been eclipsed by communication. We might wonder if we can ever find that place of tender relating with God. Instead of a love story, a life of mere communication is a frustrating, businesslike arrangement. It breeds legalism and strict codes that squeeze the life out of our union with Christ. A story from the desert fathers provides a glimpse of our choices—frustration or fire:

> Abbot Lot came to Abbot Joseph and said: Father, according as I am able, I keep my little rule, and my little fast, my prayer, meditation and contemplative silence; and according as I am able I strive to cleanse my heart of thoughts: now what more should I do? The elder rose up in reply and stretched out his hands to heaven, and his fingers became like ten lamps of fire. He said: Why not be totally changed into fire?[5]

The faithful disciple in this anecdote has the only kind of relationship with God possible within the parameters of communication: a contractual one based on moral obligations and spiritual legalities. Such polite religion excels in checking off a list of dos and don'ts, building big churches, and preaching well-written sermons. It looks good; it acts right. But it creates what Paul calls the ministry that brings death.

Abbot Joseph called Abbot Lot to something more, to not just know about spiritual fire but to become it. And the mentor's question must become ours. Why not be completely transformed into fire? More pointedly, Do you want to be transformed into fire? Do you desire to plunge into the unmanageable ardor of the Almighty God, seared to the soul, lost in the heat of God's passion that consumes you from the inside out?

The truth is, most people don't.

Such a change seems too unsafe, too out of control. But the

way of communion is the way of fire with a God who intends nothing less than communion at its most profound. Certainly God communicates directives, but most of all he desires faithful communion, which conveys words of love and mercy that can only be caught by the ear of the heart. Richard Foster beautifully reminds us of God's tremendous—almost reckless—passion toward his creation: "Today the heart of God is an open wound of love. He aches over our distance and preoccupation. He mourns that we do not draw near to him. He grieves that we have forgotten him. He weeps over our obsession with muchness and manyness. He longs for our presence."[6]

Do you know this God? Not just in your mind but in the way two people who are committed in love encounter each other? Some of you may have given up on the idea that this kind of relationship with God is possible. Perhaps you have devastated yourself by seeking communion in places of sin. Others of you are dedicated to following religious codes but, for all your performance, have only tasted the steel rigidity of rules, not the abundance that Jesus promised. I have a word for all of you: *there is another place and it is within your reach.* The banquet table is set: "Come, all you who are thirsty, come to the waters; and you who have no money, come, buy and eat!" Perhaps your spiritual journey has been scarred by disappointment, constricted by legalism, or poisoned by bitterness because the faith you were handed made this God seem distant and unattainable. It doesn't matter what happened when you were in the far country. No questions will be asked. God just wants you to come home.

The good news is that the transformation you need entails no Herculean effort on your part, no numerous promises to do better or try harder. Striving will, in fact, dismantle what God desires to do. So you can quit beating your head against a spiritual brick wall. Jesus knows you're tired, he sees your poverty, and he says, "Come to me, all you who are weary and burdened, and I will give you rest" (Matt. 11:28). While not relying on your effort, true spiritual formation does require your intent—a simple opening of the will toward God.

Thus, to find the heart's true home is to answer the call to a certain type of life. In Paul's intercession for the Ephesians, he calls them not to a particular behavior but to a way of living: "And I pray that you, being rooted and established in love, may have power, together with all the saints, to grasp how wide and long and high and deep is the love of Christ, and *to know this love that surpasses knowledge*—that you may be filled to the measure of all the fullness of God" (3:17–19, italics added). We need a new posture, a new openness to life and to the Lord of Life. The promise of Paul's prayer will never be accomplished if we are only reservoirs of spiritual facts, containers of biblical doctrine. Experiential love is the language of communion, something the intellect safeguards and reinforces but cannot replace.

Communion calls to our hearts this very moment. Will we accept the invitation to receive God's all-consuming passion in our small, wayward hearts, to allow our lives to be a living expression of that one ultimate love? The astounding truth is that our "yes" matters to God. That we love the Great Lover with the same turbulent, risky affection that he lavishes upon us is of ultimate importance—the life he aches to give us pivots on our reception of such love. He opens himself to our response now.

And so he waits. He waits.

2

DISCOVERING THE HEART'S WAY

Is it not true that for most of us who call ourselves Christians there is no real experience? We have substituted theological ideas for an arresting encounter, we are full of religious notions, but our great weakness is that for our hearts there is no one there. Whatever else it embraces, true Christian experience must always include a genuine encounter with God.
Without this, religion is but a shadow, a reflection of reality, a cheap copy of an original once enjoyed by someone else of whom we have heard.
—A. W. Tozer

Taste and see that the LORD is good.
—Psalm 34:8

When I was very young, I left pennies on my windowsill for God. I'd lined up the coins just inside the screen as if such an action were a logical way to intersect the divine. I suppose I used pennies because they were of some earthly value, and I suppose the windowsill because that would make it easier for God to swoop down to fetch them. In the morning, I'd arise to see if the pennies remained, to see if a heavenly visitation had whispered through my room during the night. The coins sat undisturbed, but I had touched upon a wonder—the idea of a God who could be wooed into my world.

Looking back, I realize that even as a child I craved for God to push past abstraction and become someone I could taste and touch in my everyday life. This small, prayerful act asked, "Does where I am matter? Can you come close?" I desired a tangible expression of God that lifted me beyond Sunday school flannelgraph lessons. I needed something bigger. I needed to feel his actual being in my living, to own the Unmanageable and be owned at the same time. I needed my story and God's story to become one.

In my child's mind, I hoped the pennies would attract his attention, pull his heart toward mine, and draw eternity into my story beyond Sunday, beyond my dime in the offering plate, beyond mere cognition.

The row of coins was a language for something I had no words to express: the hunger for communion.

I didn't understand then that God's revelation is received as either communication or communion, and that, as discussed earlier, full relationship with God engages two distinct postures— the head and the heart. The head-centered and the heart-centered postures are ways of opening to God, two differing yet complementary ways of receiving, knowing, becoming grounded in, and responding to God in holy friendship.[1] What is meant by the head and heart postures?

The last chapter discussed how the head and heart each process distinct types of stimulus in our lives, such as ideas and experiences. Ideas and experiences create different imprints upon our internal landscape, imprints that inform and shape who we are and how we see the world. Because the head and heart each process life uniquely, both postures are needed in order to discover fullness and completeness in our relationship with God.

An analogy might illustrate the way the head and heart are distinct yet interdependent. If you need to pass a difficult math exam, you spend hours poring over your notes, rereading the textbook, and practicing equations. You assume an intellectual posture of study. On the other hand, perhaps during the following week you have an important track meet. You don't read a book about running; you must experience running daily, building up muscle mass and your cardiovascular system. Here, you assume a posture of physical training.

Although these mental and physical activities are distinct, they support and inform each other. Mental preparation and balance are important for athletes, just as physical wellness creates better grounding and energy for intellectual pursuits. A person who desires to be well rounded will not choose one posture to the exclusion of the other. Such a choice would be foolish because we are not simply intellectual beings any more than we are only physical beings.

In the same way that the physical and intellectual postures need each other, the mind and heart postures must combine, reinforcing each other as the way for human beings to know God. In most evangelical circles, we are taught to pursue God by freely engaging the head posture while all but ignoring the heart posture. Thus, we find ourselves unaware of the heart's way of knowing or unsure of how to engage it. In an ideal world, the head and heart postures should be united. To even speak of them separately is misleading; everything we receive and do spiritually should naturally engage both the head and the heart. But the model for most Christians has been to shut down their hearts in the spiritual arena.

Each element of the head-focused posture has its heart-centered complement, and both are meant to reside in the lives of all Christians to the degree God calls forth. With both in operation, the believer receives fully and responds deeply. The differences between these two ways of relating to God can be summarized in the following chart:

HEAD CENTERED	HEART CENTERED
Receives God through	**Receives God through**
Intellect	Imagination
"Knowing" is contained in	**"Knowing" is contained in**
Ideas/Concepts	Experience/Emotion
Grounded in	**Grounded in**
Willingness to do	Willingness to be
Response to God	**Response to God**
Gives	Receives
Speaks	Listens
Initiates	Rests

HEAD ◄───► *BALANCE* ◄───► **HEART**

When I was younger, my relationship with God was housed exclusively on the left side of the chart. Early on, I learned how to think about God, how to analyze, how to speak out and initiate for the Lord, how to be a doer of the Word. Such was my head-centered faith. No other options were offered. So I studied the Bible, set up chairs for Sunday school, dropped in my tithe. In short, my spiritual life revolved around the head-centered posture, where God was sought through thoughts and actions of the intellect.

Are such activities bad? Certainly not. But as my journey became more and more centered on my thirst for communion, I found that the practices that characterized my life of faith only reinforced my head-centered assent to God. How could I engage God with my whole self? I started to cherish things that had historically not been of value to me. I took the spotlight off the intellect and slowly invited my heart, with its unique know-ing, into my spiritual disciplines and the life surrounding them. It was as if I discovered a second wing, small and feeble, that began to lift in concert with the other, just as God intended. With both wings—head and heart—working together, my flight of faith would never again be the same.

The Power of the Imagination

Finley Eversole notes that at age five, 90 percent of children measure in the high creativity category. Within two years, that number drops to 10 percent. By the time we reach adulthood, only 2 percent of us register as having high creativity.[2] Once we've outgrown crayons, the imagination—the stuff of creativity—is denigrated, marginalized, and considered unworthy of our time. As a creative writing teacher, my task is all the more difficult because my students have little idea of how to express themselves in imaginative ways. They have little trouble analyzing literature, but creating it is quite another matter.

Closing off the imagination is to entomb a blessed, God-given faculty that is meant to be a window of relationship with the Lord. Imagination receives God by seeing with the eyes of the heart, by allowing the Lord to come to us through symbol, images, and metaphor. Thus, the imagination has an esteemed and necessary place in the life of the believer. Still, it is considered highly suspect in many Christian circles.

The root of such suspicion lies in a response to culture, not Scripture. Christian culture seems to have experienced a misunderstanding of the imagination, viewing it as a slippery slope into potential wickedness and certainly not as a necessary spiritual faculty. The intellect is just as subject to misuse as is the imagination, yet we do not advocate silencing our analytical powers because they might be snared for evil purposes. In the same way, the imagination should not be shunned out of a fear of its ungodly potential, a stance that lacks an assurance of God's sovereignty and goodness.

But the question we must ask is, "Do we need an imaginative element in our life of faith?" Our tendency is to see imagination as an extra, the friend who gets to go on the trip with us if there's room in the car when everything else is packed. Such an attitude is a mistake. The imagination is as legitimate and necessary a faculty in our relationship with God as is the intellect. Imagination is our capacity to form concepts and images about things not physically present. Since the spiritual realm is, after all, *spiritual*, this would seem a helpful capacity. Leanne Payne, who has done excellent work on this topic, talks about true imagination as "the way we as creaturely receivers 'see' and 'hear' the inaudible, the invisible. It involves our loving and receiving from God, and from all that He has made and calls good."[3] She defines an experience of this type:

> The truly imaginative experience is defined therefore as an intuition of the real. It is an acknowledgment of objective realities (those outside the self) in their transcendent, unseen dimension (perhaps we could say, in their essence). It is that which, when received, enlarges and completes us, for it speaks to and unites with some lonely facet of our own being. All true worship, knowledge, and art come out of this. At its highest level, the truly imaginative experience (intuition of the real) is the experience of receiving from God, whether by word, vision, or (greatest of all) an infilling of Himself.[4]

Scripture is certainly full of people who, through true imaginative experience, have received from God intuitions of spiritual reality. Elisha prayed that his frightened servant would see the armies of God, and "he looked and saw the hills full of horses and chariots of fire all around Elisha" (2 Kings 6:17). Peter's vision of the sheet and the animals led him to bring the gospel to the Gentiles, and Paul's miraculous conversation with the risen Jesus altered him forever.

But the true imaginative experience also occurs in less spectacular ways. Payne asserts that even the sense of awe that captures us, such as might come during worship or while viewing grand natural beauty or great art, is our imagination receiving a sense of God's greatness and the profundity of our own lives in Christ. These are all examples of experiencing spiritual reality by "seeing" and "hearing" with the heart's imaginative faculty, that is, in a heart-centered posture.

Many spiritual materialists in the evangelical camp would deny such experiences to today's believers. But such people would be shortsighted to assume that God no longer pulls back the corner of physical reality, allowing us imaginative impressions of that which is purely spiritual. Those impressions can happen in very small ways—a picture seen in prayer, a prompting of concern to call someone; such things are ways for the heart to receive from the Lord. In *My Utmost for His Highest,* Oswald Chambers says, "The starvation of the imagination is one of the most fruitful sources of exhaustion and sapping in a worker's life. If you have not used your imagination to put yourself before God, begin to do it now. . . . Imagination is the greatest gift God has given us and it ought to be devoted entirely to Him."[5]

Faith without an element of imagination is crippled. Kathleen Norris quotes an Anglican bishop who believes, "Imagination and faith are the same thing, 'giving substance to our hopes and reality to the unseen.'"[6] While the bishop's thoughts may go a little too far, they bring up a potent idea—the necessary relationship between imagination and faith.

I can't help but wonder if part of the lackluster faith in Christian circles is not due in part to an unwillingness to honor the imagination. Hope must contain an imaginative element since "hope that is seen is no hope at all" (Rom. 8:24). Thus, in order to stand firm in any apparently hopeless situation, both the intellect and the imagination must be able to conceive of God's potential action and veiled goodness. Even the fear of death—which, even in believers, no amount of mental dogma seems able to cure—is tied to an inability to picture, to intuit, heaven.

When all else fails, both head and heart must be active in order to hold onto the unseen world, to receive completely from God. And we must discern if verses such as 2 Corinthians

4:18 are simply figurative or whether they are to be taken on some literal level: "So we fix our eyes not on what is seen, but on what is unseen. For what is seen is temporary, but what is unseen is eternal."

Symbol, Metaphor, and the Heart's Language

People love symbols. Symbols are a function of being human—we are always looking for likenesses, for comparisons, to help us frame and understand our world. Red hearts and red roses symbolize love. Black armbands symbolize mourning. White wedding dresses symbolize purity. Aside from the symbols that we as a culture share collectively, as individuals we possess personal symbols. A friend of mine seems to find a feather at pivotal moments, and these feathers have come to symbolize change in her life. One function of the imagination is to make and use symbols. Symbols—images that intimate another reality and stand in for it—are part of the heart's language.

Although as Christians we may try to deny it, human beings need symbols. Most evangelical churches completely ignore the power and potential of the symbolic. The Protestant congregations of my past seem to have suffered from a knee-jerk reaction to Catholicism, a reaction that has nearly eliminated all symbols of redemption from our places of worship. Just as receiving the bread and the wine during communion—certainly one of the church's most potent and stable symbols—has within that symbolism the possibility of a unique encounter with the living Christ, so too can other symbols spiritually charge and enrich our faith.

The symbolic certainly matters to God. The exacting construction of the ark of the covenant, the temple's architecture in Jerusalem, the snake upon the pole, the ceremonial water to cleanse the priests—all these are God-ordained symbols within the Bible, the physical that is meant to open us to blessed qualities of God.

Symbol uniquely invites all that we are—head and heart—into

spiritual reality. Symbolism is so vital that Alan Jones notes, "When symbols die, we die too."[7] Redemptive symbols—the spiritual reflected in the temporal—minister to the heart in a way dogma cannot, cleansing it of the worldly symbols with which we're bombarded in the marketplace. And it is imperative that we have godly symbols at work in our lives. Payne notes, "When a sound symbolic system . . . is missing, a lesser one takes its place. When great and good symbolic images of God, the cosmos, fatherhood, motherhood, masculine, feminine, and so on are rejected or are simply absent from the psyche, then lesser images (and even entire symbolic systems) develop to take their place. . . . We have a way of becoming (in a sense) what we set our eyes upon."[8] The cultivation of redemptive symbols is significant in healing the schism between the head and the heart.

Scripture clearly encourages us to approach God with an imaginative, heart-centered posture through not only symbol but also metaphor. The use of metaphor is rampant in the Old and New Testaments. And why? Because faith is not merely a set of ideas in need of apprehension; it is a life that is meant to engage all that we are. I have amassed a personal storehouse of metaphoric images that have become treasured gems in my vision of who God is:

> . . . like an eagle that stirs up its nest and hovers over its young, that spreads its wings to catch them and carries them on its pinions. The Lord alone led him. (Deuteronomy 32:11–12)

> "In that day," declares the LORD, "you will call me 'my husband'; you will no longer call me 'my master.'" (Hosea 2:16)

> He tends his flock like a shepherd: He gathers the lambs in his arms and carries them close to his heart; he gently leads those that have young. (Isaiah 40:11)

My prayer life has been greatly enhanced by rich images such as these. And not just by the idea of them. Certainly, God as protector and defender is a profound truth. But something within me is enlivened when I not only read about God as the loving shepherd, but I meditate on that image of a helpless lamb held against God's chest. And, with the Lord's help, entering into that metaphor, to be that lamb—and I mean *really*—is a wonder, a place of spiritual awe and unspeakable love.

Jesus' appeal to the imagination through metaphor was certainly his preferred way of inviting his listeners into the marvels of his Father's kingdom. The kingdom of God is like a mustard seed, yeast, a hidden treasure, a net laden with fish, a royal wedding banquet, and ten virgins meeting their bridegrooms. Believers are to be salt and light, a city set upon a hill, trees that bear good fruit, and branches that cling to the life-sustaining vine. God's heart for the lost is like a shepherd who leaves the sheep pen to find the one lost lamb, like a woman who feverishly searches for the missing coin, and like a wronged father who, with delirious joy, welcomes home the profligate son.

And the truth of the heart-centered posture is this: We cannot understand God, or enter into relationship with him, apart from metaphor. What attracts us to new life in Christ? Generally, it's a series of comparisons—metaphors—that we accept as reality: God as the good shepherd, the loving father, our closest friend, our beloved spouse. Without such metaphors, the footholds at the starting line of faith offer no grip.

Metaphor and symbol, and the images that accompany them, tack down the edges of our spiritual life. Without, for example, the wondrous images of God as father, shepherd, eagle, all we have is abstraction. The Bible reveals the full personality of Jesus by giving him over a hundred metaphorical names: lion, lamb, bridegroom, strong tower, cornerstone, the way, dayspring, light, lily of the valley, bright morning star. Psalm 19 asserts, "The heavens declare the glory of God; the skies proclaim the work of his hands. . . . Their voice goes out into all the earth, their words to the ends of the world" (vv. 1, 4). God created a physical world and placed us in it, and every part of our day is filled with tactile experiences that beckon us into relationship with God.

Jesus, along with the other authors of the Bible, unashamedly relied on the heart's imaginative faculties to interpret truth completely and accurately. Leland Ryken states the argument well:

> They [Jesus and the writers of the Bible] operated on the literary premise that the imagination ("imagemaking") serves as a powerful vehicle for expressing truth. They were not afraid of the indirection of metaphor or symbol, even though these literary forms require the interpretation of a reader to complete their meaning. In comparing God to a shepherd, for example, the Psalmist trusted his readers to draw the right conclusions about what God is like. . . . Most people in our culture equate reason with the abstract intellect, with concepts and propositions, but when God reasons with his people, he speaks in image, metaphor, and paradox.[9]

Whether with seed on rocky soil or lilies dancing in the fields, Jesus stresses how essential are imaginative, heart-centered ways of knowing for recognizing God and for understanding his kingdom. He presented the abstract ideas of heaven dressed in the clothing of earth. Symbols, metaphors, and images enliven and deepen our faith.

The point of examining these elements is not to embrace imagination over intellect but to recognize both. Each way of knowing God is essential. When the message of God is received by both head and heart, we find completeness in our relating with God, and we ourselves become completed in Spirit and in truth.

Experience and Emotion

Most of you who have been Christians since childhood can remember reveling in a "mountaintop" experience with God. Perhaps it was the last night of summer camp with counselors giving a soul-piercing meditation around a crackling fire. Or a special speaker who unveiled God in a fresh way, and with each word spoken you felt the lid of your heart mysteriously opened. Maybe it was a unique moment in worship when a certain song—maybe one you'd heard many times—suddenly shouted your heart's cry as the words burned in your spirit.

These are ways that God comes to you, encounters that help complete the unfolding story of your life in Christ. When the revelation of God is received through the intellect, that revelation is contained in ideas and concepts. When the revelation of God is received through the imagination, that revelation is contained in experience and emotion. The imagination becomes the catalyst for an experience with God that is as real and transforming as any physical human exchange. And through that experience of God—whether brought on through prayer, Scripture reading, or the ordinary in-breaks of the Spirit in daily life—an imprint is engraved upon your spirit that is powerful and unlike that which is impressed through the intellect. It is one thing to intellectually understand that God loves all people, including you, but it is quite another to imaginatively receive the love of God whispered to your heart.

You can go beyond knowing *about* the love of God, good as that is, to also *experiencing* the love of God. Both of these ways of knowing God are essential. Many of us can recount experiences wherein we've felt the life of God roar into an ordinary moment, causing a highly emotional response that drew us into a deeper place of intimacy and relating. Such powerful intersections with God are generally notable for their intensity as well as their rarity.

But are they meant to be rare? Certainly the elevated passion of such moments is not meant to be constant—it would soon wear us out! We point to such times on our spiritual maps as important landmarks, which they are. But too often we have no daily experience of God that connects the various spots on the map. It seems we don't expect God to anchor himself in mundane moments of daily life. Christ is constantly present, and each moment holds the seeds of encounter. Yet much of the time, we miss him.

For most Christians, God is an abstraction, a big balloon of virtue, floating by whenever we have our devotions. When Jesus says, "And surely I will be with you always, even to the very end of the age," we don't take it very literally. We consistently underestimate the presence of Jesus in the now and, at the level of daily living, he is often lost. The truth that waits to tear like a cyclone through our complacency is this: "The Christ of faith is no less accessible to us in His present risenness than was the Christ of history in His human flesh."[10] Dare we believe this? How different would our lives be if we responded to this truth with our ordinary living?

There's no substitute for experiencing firsthand the goodness of Jesus. Luke 19 records the story of Zacchaeus, cheating tax collector extraordinaire. He was likely familiar with reports of Jesus' radical teaching, his preference for the disenfranchised, and his healings. Such information—or maybe just a desire to hop on the bandwagon—prompted Zacchaeus to secure a balcony seat in the sycamore for the parade. But the procession paused unexpectedly under that tree, and Jesus declared, "Zacchaeus, come down immediately. I must stay at your house today." By that statement Jesus meant that he wanted to enter into intimate friendship with Zacchaeus. After sharing a meal with Jesus, Zacchaeus erupted into euphoria, babbling about returning quadruple the amount of money he had swindled from others. Zacchaeus was utterly transformed into a new and passionate person, a man suddenly dedicated to doing the right thing. Neither knowledge of Jesus' teaching nor playing the cool observer loosened the purse strings that chained this man's impoverished soul. A personal experience with the incredible

Lord of life sparked new life in Zacchaeus. So, too, is it with us all.

One summer I welcomed a visitor from my graduate school days. Dan and I were good friends during those years, and we were leaders in campus ministry. As students searching for the deeper things of God, we belonged to a group that regularly gathered for long spiritual discussions while sharing boxed macaroni and cheese after church or while sipping coffee in the student union. While our contact was minimal during the years since, he didn't hesitate to call when he passed through my part of the country. But our few days together were not what I had hoped. We spent time catching up on our lives and news of mutual friends, yet it seemed difficult for me to steer the conversation in the direction of our spiritual lives. My life with God was exciting and freeing—an intimacy had opened. My enthusiasm was matched only by Dan's apparent apathy.

Once Dan had left town, I pondered with God the difference between us. I was genuinely perplexed. Dan knew Jesus, had bent his knee to him and accepted him as Savior. So why, I asked God, did my spirit feel like the well-watered garden, the spring of water never ceasing that Isaiah talks about, and Dan's seemed parched? I certainly didn't have more Jesus than Dan did. What made the difference?

I eventually got my answer. Yes, Dan and I both knew the same Jesus, *but I was experiencing the Jesus I knew.* In my worship, my Bible reading, my drive to work, I was experiencing my Lord—expecting him, welcoming him. My relationship with God had a tangibility that seemed absent for Dan. In short, I had received God's love in both head and heart—first as fact, then as encounter. That's what made the difference. That's where the passion came from. And that's where true spiritual passion always comes from.

The pendulum of Christian opinion swings wide in regard to experience and emotion. At one end, head-centered culture often scorns emotionality and sniffs at those who desire an encounter with God. Emotionality and a desire for experience, they believe, threatens true and abiding faith and weakens the head-centered, intellectual posture, which is singularly capable of navigating the rough waters of life. This stance, however, is sterile and severely hobbles the second component of knowing God, the heart-centered posture, or heart's way of knowing.

On the other extreme are those who are overly attached to emotionality and experience. For some the wrung hanky is proof that the Holy Spirit stopped by for tea and scones. Emotionality becomes a barometer of spirituality. We cannot, however, chase emotional experiences with God and desire God himself in the same moment. To become intent upon "achieving" some fervent emotional connection with God misses the mark. God alone must always be the focus and never a mere by-product of relationship with him. Says Leanne Payne, "It is a mistake to pursue experience, to desire 'high impact' encounters. There is such a thing as *spiritual lust*."[11]

Both stances—shunning and overattachment—tend to objectify emotions and experience, making them tools to achieve a desired outcome that will sate our fears or the ego-driven self. In the center of the pendulum's arc lies a measured response where emotional experience can be seen for what it is: one necessary piece that joins with others to create a complete relationship with the Lord.

The Gift of Being

The story is told of three desert fathers who traveled regularly to visit Anthony, a venerable old spiritual guide. Two of the three men always engaged Anthony in lively conversation on matters of the soul while the third sat silent. Eventually, Anthony said to the third man, "You often come here to see me, but you never ask me anything," to which the third man replied, "It is enough to see you, Father."[12]

We treasure rare individuals like Anthony, who "do" ministry simply by their presence, quietly exuding the fragrance of Christ. The compassion of God is etched into their faces and

engraved upon their hands, making their slightest gesture powerful. In their lives with Jesus, such people balance the head-
centered posture of doing with the heart's way of simply being.
So, too, can your imaginative reception of the Lord and his
Word create a strong sense of being within your soul and in
your presence to others.

As a person raised in a typical church setting, my Christianity was highly intellectual. I learned how to apply myself to
godly activities. I believed the way to be in relationship with
God was to initiate disciplines, to work, to serve—in short, to
keep doing. I knew of no other way to approach God, and even
if I sensed a hollowness within this approach, the remedy was
to keep striving. While there is nothing inherently negative about
spiritual action—indeed, we need it—I was only taught how to
do for God, never how to just *be* with God. Sören Kirkegaard
once lamented, "We have forgotten how to be. We can only
talk about being." I received no models for how to simply be
with God. So as I grew and matured in Christ, there was no
being behind my doing.

Having a layer of being undergirding doing is essential for
all authentic disciples of Christ. Spiritually speaking, we can
only give away what we've received. The heart's way is the key
to cultivating the being that deepens and dignifies our doing
and raises it as a sweet offering to the Lord. It is vital to create
moments to simply be. We need time for receiving, for listening, for simply reveling in the fact that we are loved because we
are and not for any spiritual product we might generate. Without the balance of being, we will have precious little to offer
the hurting community around us. What we'll possess is a thin
layer of good, moral behavior that has no true substance. We
need being.

And isn't a sense of being the essential quality that separates
our actions from unbelievers? Except for evangelism, which an
unbeliever would naturally not engage in, there is no activity a
Christian does that claims any uniqueness. People who refuse
Christ can ladle up soup for the hungry, distribute clothes to

the poor, build houses for the destitute, and operate health clinics in Third World countries. To use Thomas Merton's metaphor, what distinguishes the Christian's initiation into the river of activity is the still lake of being that feeds it. We require times immersed in the lake of being where that silent, radiant quality of God's presence beautifies our action in the world, refreshing and replenishing the river of our daily doing.

We must take seriously our need to cultivate being, which means space must be created for it in our disciplines as well as in our living. Luke 10 gives us a picture of what the state of the Christian soul is intended to be:

> As Jesus and his disciples were on their way, he came to a village where a woman named Martha opened her home to him. She had a sister called Mary, who sat at the Lord's feet listening to what he said. But Martha was distracted by all the preparations that had to be made. She came to him and asked, "Lord, don't you care that my sister has left me to do the work by myself? Tell her to help me!" "Martha, Martha," the Lord answered, "you are worried and upset about many things, but only one thing is needed. Mary has chosen what is better, and it will not be taken away from her" (vv. 38–42).

Mary, enthralled with the Lord's presence, forgets the commotion clattering around her, intent on hanging her heart upon Jesus' every word. For this sacred moment, there is no doing, only being. When asked to rebuke Mary, Jesus not only refuses, he states that she has chosen what is most essential since "only one thing is needed."

Only one thing is needed. How many of us take these words of Jesus as a literal command, as an expression of what is good and right in our own lives?

The truth is, we tend to identify with Martha, not Mary. We are caught in habitual, if not addictive, patterns of busyness. We are constantly drawn to activity, and we are often restless, even fearful, in moments of quiet. Even while we acknowledge that Mary's posture—the heart's way of being with Jesus—is necessary, we tend to model our lives after the ever-active Martha. And like her, we are often critical of those in the church whom we believe are not doing enough—perhaps because their willingness to be unmasks the superficiality of compulsive activity.

People for whom busyness is a primary way of relating to the Lord may wonder if centering one's self in being isn't just an excuse for getting out of scooping up tuna casserole at the church dinner. These busy people are tempted to view being time as a type of spiritual navel gazing that might create a *laissez faire* attitude toward serving. A focus on being, they might argue, has little practicality in a world where the fields are white unto harvest. In fact, the opposite is true. In the economy of God, as Tim Hansel has pointed out, addictive busyness is the greatest form of spiritual laziness possible. A sense of being and all that accompanies it are part of our spiritual responsibility and so vital to the life of the Spirit. Discovering quiet, still places in our lives with the Lord, moments that overflow into our activities, is part of the calling of every believer. Those places of being are found at the feet of Jesus, and those believers whose service is rooted in the ground of being are the church's most effective servants.

The Heart Responds

So the choice of Mary remains: to rest at the Lord's feet, listening, loving, receiving—letting dinner wait, letting the dishes pile up. The intimate posture of Mary toward Jesus strummed the innermost strings of his heart. Still, Mary and Martha are, after all, sisters: when the awe and stillness of Mary becomes integrated into our Martha-esque lives—melding both doing and being into a continuous spiritual response to Jesus—the heart then receives, listens to, and rests in the Lord, even amid the busyness of the kitchen. These three elements—receiving, listening, resting—are connected and constitute the fruits of the heart's way. Most Christians, however, find these fruits to be foreign.

As westernized Christians, we're adept at giving to God. We hear in various and subtle ways, "What have you given to the Lord lately?" But how often do we hear, "How are you receiving from the Lord right now?" We're impoverished when it comes to receiving what he desires to give to us. Yet it is only in receiving from God that we possess anything of substance to give away.

Not long ago, I bantered with a group of students before class about the command to love others. "What do you do," I asked them, "when you find yourself stressed out and cranky with everyone you meet? How do you love then?" Their strategy could be summed up in two words: try harder! Pray harder, study your Bible more, will yourself to love. In short, do more. Their answer sounded tiring to me and of limited usefulness besides, so I tossed in what appeared for many to be a new thought: If your interactions contain no expressions of God's love, then your thirsty soul requires the stillness where that one love can be received. Sacred space is the thing most needed since we only radiate love received. Afterward, I spoke with one student who agreed with what I'd said but was clearly perplexed, even sorrowful. "I want to know God in a deeper way and receive from him," she said, "but I don't know what it means to receive from God or how to do that."

I understood what she meant because rarely have I encountered a Sunday school class or sermon on how to hear God or to receive from him, which is a grievous misfortune, because in order to receive we must first be able to listen. The idea of prayerfully listening to God as a serious spiritual discipline never occurred to me until I was nearly thirty. A number of ways can be employed for listening to the Lord: Bible reading (this way of listening is not automatic—one must approach Scripture as an exercise in listening, rather than solely as intellectual enlightenment), the counsel of godly people, and personally intuiting the voice of God as it comes.

In John 10, Jesus uses the metaphor of the shepherd and the sheep pen to describe how his followers hear and heed his voice because they "know" it. They flee from the unfamiliar voice of the stranger. Sadly, many Christians today are overly concerned about misinterpreting the voice of God. They give Satan more credit in his quest to distort than they give to God in his ability to make himself clearly heard. Neglecting to listen and to receive in their spiritual lives leaves such believers adrift, like sailors navigating without instruments, unable to discern the voice of God through the heart's stillness.

The life of Jesus certainly models the rhythm of receiving and giving, listening and speaking, resting and acting. The Gospels repeatedly tell us how Jesus sought out lonely and deserted places to pray. Luke 21:37–38 says, "Each day Jesus was teaching at the temple, and each evening he went out to spend the night on the hill called the Mount of Olives, and all the people came early in the morning to hear him at the temple." Why did Jesus not stay in Jerusalem where the accommodations were surely more comfortable and convenient? One likely reason was the opportunity for rest, a rest removed from the clamoring crowds and noise of the city, in a hidden place where he could open himself to uncluttered listening and receiving from his Father. Here, we see how the three responses—listening, receiving, resting—interconnect. His retreat, then, to the Mount of Olives (and other "lonely" places described in Scripture) fostered a hiddenness of heart where these three elements were not an interruption of his ministry but, rather, the lifeblood of it. Out of this sacred place of being, Jesus was able to return to the crowds the next day and to say, "For I did not speak of my own accord, but the Father who sent me commanded me what to say and how to say it" (John 12:49).

Each of us is called to our own Mount of Olives, those hidden places that forsake the crowds that compete for our attention day by day. Without those places, we forfeit fullness, and our lives live us, not the other way around. The disciplines of resting, listening, and receiving are not optional in the life of the Spirit, because we will never plumb the depths of Christ without honoring these dimensions of spirituality.

More Pennies

I got over the need to leave pennies on the windowsill as a way to invite God into my world. But I never got over the need to invite God to be an intimate part of my world.

When was the last time you offered an invitation of spiritual currency, throwing open the window to your heart? Without a sense of God in our daily experience, in our actual living, we possess an unnamable sense of absence. And this is not true only of Christians but of all of humanity, saint and sinner alike. Thomas Merton talks about our inbred yearning for God: "To desire God is the most fundamental of all human desires. It is the very root of all our quest for happiness. Even the sinner, who seeks happiness where it cannot be found, is following a blind, errant desire for God which is not aware of itself. So that, from one point of view, it is impossible not to desire God."[13] The God whom our passions would enfold couldn't be more ours. He is the end of all our hungers. But he must be sought with the whole self; we must take as gospel Jesus' charge, "Love the Lord your God with all your heart and with all your soul and with all your mind and with all your strength" (Mark 12:30).

Even as we endeavor to follow Christ with head and heart, with all that we are and hope to be, there will be times of desert, moments of struggle, hours of despair. We are called to a life, a whole life, one that imitates Christ both in his joy and in his suffering. And we are called to obedience, to pursue God and love him with the sum total of our being. But how can we do this? God fashioned both head and heart as portals to heaven, as thoroughfares of communication and communion. The intellect has long been on a human-made pedestal, fashioned by the chisels of culture. But the Lord desires that, in all our moments with him, our hearts become present so that all we are may be opened to relationship with Christ.

To be complete, that relationship needs engagement of both head and heart. Trying to know God with only one or the other is like a bird attempting to fly with only one wing. It might flutter off the ground a bit, stir up a little dust, but without both wings working together it will never soar into the heavenly realms. Embrace the second half of your spiritual self and merge both ways of relating to God through fully realizing the heart's intimate pathway. You are, after all, created for flight, to fully live, to fully experience doing and being in that beautiful place poised between heaven and earth, where your story becomes God's and God's story forever yours.

3

UNMASKING THE
FALSE SELF

*Those who live according to the sinful nature have their minds
set on what that nature desires; but those who live in accordance
with the Spirit have their minds set on what the Spirit desires.
The mind of the sinful man is death, but the mind controlled by
the Spirit is life and peace.*
—Paul the Apostle *(Romans 8:5–6)*

*This new life impedes us in our natural outlook and ways until
we get these things rightly related by "putting on the new man,"
until the Son of God is formed in us and both the natural and
the holy are the same.*
—Oswald Chambers

It was a bad summer—disappointments and discord, fallout
from splintered relationships, pressures on my fractured character. Such things left me floundering in my inadequacies. And
worse yet, I looked as inadequate as I felt, my struggle plainly
evident in the display window of my life. There was no hiding

my brokenness and defects. Unable to publicly present a mask of calmness, control, and wisdom—the person I desperately desired to be—I was powerless to cloak my most despised characteristics with a veneer of competence.

One day I sat stewing on my apartment building's front steps, a personal sanctuary and think place. What was happening to me? My reactions to these painful situations and to my skewed reputation seemed out of proportion. Then one of those rare, clear conversations occurred with the God who seemed so distant from my messy dilemma.

"Do you know why you're so upset?" my heart heard him ask. The question startled me.

"No, tell me."

"You're acting as weak as you are and you can't stand it."

"Yes," I answered, a little stunned at so simple a revelation, "that's right."

Acting as weak as I am. If I am *weak, why is it so shaming for me to see myself behaving that way? Why isn't that acceptable?*

It was a good summer—I collapsed into weakness, the wreckage that I was, and quit trying to reassemble the shards of my mask. It was a crossroads. To a few people whom I trusted, I revealed my struggles and the sin—much of it *my* sin—that helped put me there. It was actually a great summer, because the self I thought was me evaporated into its own falsity. Through learning the intricacies of the phantom who craved acclaim and wore my clothes, I was able to begin a journey of knowing God more intimately.

That summer began a *metanoia*, meaning "a profound change, a conversion."

My story is far from unique. We all wrestle with fidelity to outward images while wanting to be true to the person God calls us to be. Contradictions abound. On the surface of things, the heart's way of Mary attracts us, but we cower in rooms of cold intellect. We desire a bare-skinned experience of God but knit together fig leaves. We might enjoy the thought of simply being in Christ but give ourselves over to compulsive activity.

The head/heart schism remains unbridged by spiritual self-help books, sermons, and our own spiritual self-improvement campaigns. What is at the core of our apparent inability to find healing?

A better question is *who* is at the core of this struggle.

Identity is the foundation of the journey with God, the very bedrock of the spiritual life. Identity involves how I see myself, how I view God, and how I understand life itself. All spiritual formation, every handhold to the next rung of holiness, hangs on how I resolve the question of who I really am.

Identity is always forged in and through relationships. From babyhood, our sense of self forms from interactions—how others react to us and how we respond to them. As a result, each of us possesses two basic selves: the false self and the true self. These two identities are born of the two types of relationships that we can enter into: human-centered relationships or God-centered relationship.

The persona that is built and molded in human-centered interactions is the false self. The self that was created by God and is unfolded in communion with him is the true self. The identity that we embrace determines if ours will be a life of shadow or of substance, a life celebrated in the good country of grace or an existence marked by self-imposed exile from our deepest truths. Most Christians live their whole lives as someone they're not, dedicated to an image that wears the face of a stranger. Their sense of identity is uneasy, fluctuating, lost in a struggle to believe that what God says about them is true.

An Introduction to the False Self

We all know the phony—the woman dressed to the nines with an inch of makeup; the balding, middle-aged man who drives a sports car that's worth twice the average annual salary. We sense their falseness, their desperateness to be someone else. But what about us? What about you? What is your fidelity to the self whom God created and with whom he desires to be in relationship? The truth is, each of us owns a false self, and without intervention, it will be the rudder that steers our living.

The false self is the self created outside of the mind of God, the self that seeks existence apart from God. The false self is a facade that we construct in order to gain love and acceptance in the world, a mask of counterfeit adequacy. This mask is constructed of all the characteristics and qualities that we fiercely clutch as ours and want others to believe that we possess. It is our unreal identity, controlling and defining us.

Where does this false self come from? God created us to be holy receptacles of his unconditional love. Within each of us is a beautiful spiritual self of inestimable value, loved simply because it exists, not for anything it does. But we live in a world where love is often conditional, in a culture that equates beauty with behavior and appearance. The genesis of the false self lies in childhood as a defense mechanism that protects us from the pain of not receiving the *agape*, or unconditional love, that God designed for us from the beginning. These defenses become a way to cope and can even be the key to survival for children who live in extremely dysfunctional environments. Living in an imperfect universe, we quickly learn to create responses that procure for us cheap imitations of godly love and acceptance.

The negative messages we receive from culture, parents, and other authority figures boil down to two ideas: we are irredeemably defective, and we need to earn love in order to receive love. Whether these ideas are whispered on occasion or shouted constantly, all of us have, to some degree, internalized and been wounded by such messages. To contend with these wounds, we craft a public face in order to cope, to fit in, and ultimately to find self-definition.

We quickly learn that certain actions and emotions are applauded while others are condemned. A public self rises to handle the uncertain and even capricious world in which we find ourselves. Eventually, an overidentification with these outward behaviors comprises the conscious mind's sense of identity. If, for instance, you're good at sports, your skills might form the core of how you think about yourself. If you're smart, your intelligence becomes the prime source of your identity. "That's who I am," you think, "the person who does these behaviors or performs in these roles."

The self as behavior and performance isn't biblical, of course, but except for deep healing and reformation in Christ, we will identify ourselves as a behaving self, which is always a false self. So we continue to cultivate external responses until what started as a simple, reflexive defense becomes a persona, a second self that encases the first. The false self eventually outlives its original usefulness in protecting us as children. As adults, it becomes the stubborn, painted surface of our lives.

Self and Sin

In Scripture, Paul speaks of the self that is created by our fallenness, identifying it as the "old self." The term *false self* communicates the same message but emphasizes that this type of self is a mask with no reality in the light of God's truth. Recognizing the spiritual danger inherent in the false, or old, self, Paul calls God's people to forsake this foundation of our sin nature:

> Put to death, therefore, whatever belongs to your earthly nature: sexual immorality, impurity, lust, evil desires and greed, which is idolatry. Because of these, the wrath of God is coming. You used to walk in these ways, in the life you once lived. But now you must rid yourselves of all such things as these: anger, rage, malice, slander, and filthy language from your lips. Do not lie to each other, since you have taken off your old self with its practices and have put on the new self, which is being renewed in knowledge in the image of its Creator. (Colossians 3:5–10)

You were taught, with regard to your former way of life,
to put off your old self, which is being corrupted by its
deceitful desires; to be made new in the attitude of your
minds; and to put on the new self, created to be
like God in true righteousness and holiness. (Ephesians
4:22–24)

If we have been united with him like this in his death,
we will certainly also be united with him in his resurrection. For we know that our old self was crucified with
him so that the body of sin might be done away with.
(Romans 6:5–6)

It's obvious from these passages that the struggle with the
false self is as old as humankind. In these Scriptures, Paul is
not urging non-Christians to put on the new self. Rather, he is
exhorting believers—people who had carried into their faith
life a sanitized "old man," rather than fully embracing the new
creation. Although they had verbally declared themselves as
new creatures in Christ, their continued allegiance to the old
life was spoken with every action. And we are no different. We
need to heed Paul's words and discover for ourselves the ways
in which old-self living has been dragged into our new-creation
life.

None of us, of course, advertises this allegiance to the false
self. None of us wanders about, crying, "Who am I?" We know
the right answer: I am a child of God, who unconditionally
loves me. Yet when the promotion falls through, the relationship is shipwrecked, the hoped-for change fails to materialize,
our wanderings through the emotional ruins of our lives speak
loudly of where we anchor our identity. The schism between
the head and the heart is strongly at work here: we possess
plenty of ideas about who we are in God's eyes, but those
ideas are refuted by how we function in daily situations. We
shuffle through the day, our sense of self like a pinball bounc-
ing off of any number of externals while verses about identity

in Christ trip from our lips. We are a living, breathing contradiction, aligned to God in thought but alarmingly separate in
our hearts.

This separateness creates a sense of autonomy and self-rule.
A radical individualism replaces communion with God. And
with it comes the source of all sin. Much of our difficulty with
sin is that we focus on fixing wrong actions instead of going
back to square one. We need to come face-to-face with the false
self that created the sinful motivation in the first place. James
Finley's perspective is helpful:

> The matter of *who* we are always precedes what we do.
> Thus, sin is not essentially an action but rather an iden-
> tity. Sin is a fundamental stance of wanting to be what
> we are not. Sin is an orientation to falsity, a basic lie
> concerning our own deepest reality. Likewise, inversely,
> to turn away from sin is, above all, to turn away from a
> tragic case of mistaken identity concerning our own
> selves.[1]

Fixating only on actions in a desire to deepen holiness and
sanctification misses the mark and exiles us from our God-
created selves. We do well not to be satisfied with trying harder
the next time but to ask, "Who was I trying to *be* when I chose
that sinful response?" Being precedes doing. We must not simply wrench ourselves away from sin but repent deeper by recognizing sin's foundation in identity.

Metanoia is not created by altering our behaviors—latching
onto a new method of prayer or Bible reading, signing up for
more church retreats, or pondering an innovative formula for
how to do the spiritual life. We always want the quick God-fix.
But such cosmetic alterations are the spiritual equivalent of
rearranging the deck furniture on the *Titanic*. Rather, our false-
self identity and the way it views reality must be challenged,
transformed, and finally redeemed.

The Grand Illusion

To recognize the presence of the false self, we must answer the question, "What is it like?" The false self has three elements that are cyclical in nature: it is illusory; which leads to a focus on externals; which creates a drive for esteem, power, and security; which, when possessed, reinforce the illusion. The interaction of these elements is depicted in the following diagram:

FALSE-SELF CYCLE

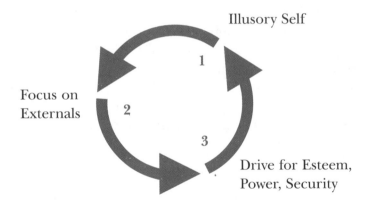

The false-self cycle is one way to understand the bondage that traps many Christians. We sense the wrongness of such a life but have few resources to free ourselves from its prison. Thus, we are reduced to shadowboxing, trying to hit something, anything, to somehow conquer that which binds us. As maturing Christians, we have the power of Christ to break the false-self cycle and make life-giving choices that will open doors of deeper, more intimate fellowship with God.

The foundational element of the false-self cycle is illusion. The false self is a mask, a collage even, of how we desire to be seen and responded to in our lives. Simply put, the false self is a lie about our real personhood, an image we dedicate ourselves to grooming for public display. Because humanity cannot in and of itself create anything substantial or eternal, this "person" is nothing more than a ghost we invite to haunt our daily consciousness. Thomas Merton's interpretation of the false self is powerful:

> Every one of us is shadowed by an illusory person: a false self. This is the man I want myself to be but who cannot exist, because God does not know anything about him. And to be unknown of God is altogether too much privacy. My false and private self is the one who wants to exist outside the reach of God's will and God's love—outside of reality and outside of life. And such a self cannot help but be an illusion. . . . But there is no substance under the things with which I am clothed. I am hollow, and my structure of pleasures and ambitions has no foundation. . . . And when they are gone there will be nothing left of me but my own nakedness and emptiness and hollowness, to tell me that I am my own mistake.[2]

When you believe that the false self is who you really are, then God can know nothing about you, because he recognizes only that which he created. The self that is perpetuated out of woundedness and wrong motives has no meaning, no substance, in the kingdom of God. Its existence is beyond fragile—held together by carefully choreographed thought patterns. It's a dance that adds up to illusion.

One problem with recognizing the illusion of the false self is that it *feels* real. This ghost has a subjective reality, meaning we sense substance, we sense tangibility—flesh and bone—around it; thus, people sincerely believe they are their false selves. But this is a delusion. Psychiatrist Gerald May reminds us that "our self-images, whatever we feel is 'me' at a given time, are in fact cellular representations of self."[3] In the world of objective reality—that which is *really* real—the false self is nothing more than an elaborate collection of cells firing within the brain. From this point of view, it is at best foolish and at worst tragic to allow a lie that is perpetrated within a little gray matter to determine who I say I am and to direct my life.

What labels, though, can be placed on true identity? What adjectives can be employed to describe our real self? Perhaps you are a good friend, spouse, student, or church worker, talented, spiritual, and humble. Or maybe you're a disappointment to others, too needy, unlikable, a huge bundle of flaws. The list goes on. Yet how many of these things are really you or really me? Are they substance or shadow? Certainly within our minds they seem real, but the ultimate question is whether these labels and roles mirror what God says is true about us.

The false self is the ultimate shadow, an empty and invisible entity that cannot be seen unless something external covers it. Jesus refers to the false self in Luke 13, speaking of those who align themselves with the Messiah but who do not enter the narrow door: "Once the owner of the house gets up and closes the door, you will stand outside knocking and pleading, 'Sir, open the door for us.' But he will answer, 'I don't know you or where you come from.' Then you will say, 'We ate and drank with you, and you taught in our streets.' But he will reply, 'I don't know you or where you come from'" (vv. 25–27). Why couldn't the owner of the house, who is Jesus, recognize people who so clearly recognized him? If we call ourselves disciples but do not embrace the identity that Christ fashioned and died for, not even attempts to jog God's memory will be of any help to us. Part of what it means to enter through the narrow door is to cast aside the camouflage of the false self, the person Jesus cannot acknowledge because it does not exist.

A Superficial Focus

Because no internal machinations maintain the false self, the second element in the false-self cycle is a focus on externals. The false self must always be doing, always moving, but limiting everything it does and encounters to a superficial level.

To peer beneath the shell, to look at how things really are, is terrifying.

All of us, to one degree or another, experience the pull of compulsive activity. It becomes hard to slow down. An uncomfortable emptiness occurs, an aversion to just sitting with God, and we feel pulled to produce, to perform, to plow through the next five things on the to-do list. This is the hand of the false self slowly, silently pushing us toward frenetic busyness. Our doing has become our being, and the untended garden of the inner life becomes overgrown with the tangled activities of an illusory person.

Jesus repeatedly confronted the Pharisees' insistence upon the primacy of surface behavior, actions that look glittery but only disguise the dung heap within. In Matthew 23, Jesus says of them, "You clean the outside of the cup and dish, but inside they are full of greed and self-indulgence. . . . You are like whitewashed tombs, which look beautiful on the outside but on the inside are full of dead men's bones and everything unclean. In the same way, on the outside you appear to people as righteous but on the inside you are full of hypocrisy and wickedness" (vv. 25, 27–28). Jesus clearly saw the focus on external holiness for what it was—a way to divert attention from the importance of internal issues and authentic holiness that must, by necessity, have a foundation in the heart.

Like the Pharisees, we often want to "have our cake and eat it too." We want to cultivate the appearance of holiness without having to endure any of the internal transformations that create true holiness. We settle for a false-self holiness and declare that our shallow existence is the abundant life Jesus died to give us.

The Three Drives

People are a strange bundle of motivations. Everything we do has a motive. Sometimes within Christian circles, this issue of motivation is eclipsed by a focus on producing right behavior.

But is it enough to only worry about moral activity? How much does motivation matter? And if a love for God doesn't drive behavior, what does? These questions are vital to keep in mind as the last element of the false-self cycle is explored.

The most godly motivations arise from our souls, which, in alignment with God's will, gladly choose what pleases the Lord. But with no internal motivation, the false self must be fueled by that which is outside of itself. Thus, the third element of the false-self cycle consists of three motives or drives: security, esteem, and power. As these drives are pursued in the world's arena, the illusory strength of the false self is further fortified, the cycle is perpetuated, and the false self is given legitimacy.

These three drives, as identified by Thomas Keating, need to be constantly derived from one's environment in order for the false self to fully function.[4] Why security, esteem, and power? These insatiable drives emerge out of childhood. The need for security, esteem, and power is appropriate for infants and children. Little ones must gain a sense of security from their environment, they need to be loved by their caretakers, and as they grow, they should be empowered to become separate, more autonomous beings. These major needs for infants, says Keating, are rarely met in a satisfying manner because the unconditional love of God was not received in its fullness. When these needs are not met, we, as children, experience woundedness and without healing, navigate adulthood attempting to satiate these unfulfilled drives.

Adults, too, possess a need for *healthy* security, esteem, and power. But when adulthood is spent chasing after outward emblems of security, esteem, and power, something is terribly wrong. We are compensating for childhood woundedness by living in the false self. If we do not seek the Lord as the true source of our security and love and do not entrust our lives to his power and his sovereignty, we live separated from God. The three drives can be thought of as the engine parts that enable the old self to putter down life's highway, and Christians, no less than nonbelievers, are prone to spend their energies chasing after these things. We are sometimes even more deluded because most of us give them legitimacy by labeling these drives as part of spiritual living.

In short, anytime our lives become fixed on attaining external experiences of security, esteem, and power, the false self is automatically in residence. Because of their significance in the false-self cycle, each of these drives will be examined individually.

Security and Trust

On September 10, 1946, a thirty-six-year-old woman traveled by train to Darjeeling, India. She had already served in India many years, giving up a more comfortable ministry in Europe, willing to serve the Lord at a Catholic girls' school in Calcutta. Now, on the train, Agnes Bojaxhiu, known in religious life as Teresa, faced "the call within the call." Mother Teresa writes of that moment: "The message was quite clear—I was to give up all and follow Jesus into the slums—to serve Him in the poorest of the poor. . . . I was to leave the convent and work with the poor, living among them. . . . I knew where I belonged but I did not know how to get there."[5] Without knowing if anyone would come with her or how the ministry would be run, Mother Teresa left the relative safety of the Calcutta convent to venture into the slums of India. Through her abandonment of what was safe, secure, and comfortable, along with her simple obedience to God, Mother Teresa became an icon of tireless, selfless service to others in the name of Jesus.

It would be easy to categorize such a woman as uncommon, a person who follows God in a unique way. In truth, there should be nothing special or uncommon about obedience to Christ, about following wherever he leads. But within a church culture that is absolutely absorbed in the false-self cycle, it is, unfortunately, out of the ordinary.

The false self's life is the house built upon sand (Matthew 7). Because its foundation is built upon shifting externals rather than upon God, which creates a frightening sense of instability, the false self constantly craves security from its environment. Security becomes a primary motivation, guiding many or most decisions.

Every day, people make decisions influenced by a desire for security. Ask yourself, "To what degree are my employment decisions based on money or job security? Would I willingly confront an injustice in the workplace even if it might jeopardize my job? When I consider where I should live, how much of a factor is the safety and security of the neighborhood? Do I move toward new relationships or remain in unhealthy relationships because I clutch a measure of safety or security that they provide? Have I ever refused to do something that I felt God might be calling me to do because it felt too threatening, too unsafe?"

None of us is immune to pressure from the false self to play it safe, to keep a hedge of security around us. The problem is, we become enamored with safety. When this occurs, pressing hard after the Lord's will, abandoning ourselves to the character of God, offering up livelihoods and possessions to follow Jesus are seen as too romantic and too risky. Though rarely voiced this bluntly, our fears can easily infect our motivations. We give lip service to the romantic while examining our choices through the eyes of our culture, gravitating toward those options with the most safety and security. Thus, the manner in which we make choices is virtually indistinguishable in practice from the average non-Christian's method, except for the invocation of God's name to lend legitimacy. We mimic the world, and it's simply business as usual.

One year I was suddenly laid off from my job right before Thanksgiving. I felt as though the desktop of my life, laden with the paperwork of activities, responsibilities, and busyness, had been swept clean. With little savings, I faced a winter of unemployment. I sank into a pit devoid of obvious handholds of security. Depression lingered over me like the clouds that clung to the sky that long, cold season.

I could have recited verse after verse about God as my provider, my fortress, my rock and refuge, yet when I was called upon to actually, not just mentally, affirm my trust in him, I faltered. My false self—who counted on tangible securities, who wanted faith based on sight—was shaken and exposed. With God's help, I held on to truth, wrestled with fear, and pressed through to points unknown. I ventured off the map of my known faith and many months later, began to move into true vocation for the first time in my life.

My initial struggle with security issues, though, was complicated by Christian culture's definition of faith as cognitive assent. Belief, I was taught, is about mentally digesting a series of spiritual truths. This limited definition only takes into consideration the head-centered posture, and so belief becomes a set of ideas. Thus, I mentally understood and affirmed the Lord as a good and trustworthy God, yet when I was called upon to act, to step off the cliff of my creeds, I balked.

For the heart-centered posture, the definition of faith is trust. And how is trust expressed? By moving, childlike, toward Jesus and the things he points me toward. In the Bible, when people are commended by Jesus for their faith, it comes on the heels of their physically approaching him in simple, childlike trust, not because they have mentally stored spiritual truths. Jesus applauds them for a courageous action, not an accurate idea. Conversely, as one author puts it, "When Jesus reproved the disciples for their 'lack of faith,' he meant their lack of trust and courage; it wasn't a reprimand for dropping one or another article of faith from the creed."[6] Faith blends both belief and trust—head and heart—into a complete response to Christ.

In Matthew 6, Jesus confronts the drive for outward symbols of security, rather than depending upon the goodness of God to meet human needs. In the famous "do not worry" passage, Jesus says, "Look at the birds of the air; they do not sow or reap or store away in barns, [stockpiling—certainly a good source of security in the world], and yet your heavenly Father feeds them. Are you not much more valuable than they?" (v. 26). A clear distinction is made between those who worry about the stuff of life—what to wear, eat, drink—and those who are able to live a winged life of unself-conscious trust. The false self's motivations are based on worry, since this world cannot offer perpetual security. And such worry is itself a type of prayer, paying homage to the lesser god of capricious circumstance.

To determine the degree to which your security rests in things other than God, ask yourself, "What am I afraid of?" The Gospels reveal that the Pharisees, who are emblematic of the false self, were constantly afraid of Jesus and the people over whom they ruled. They appeared powerful and unruffled, but fear reigned in all their interactions and decisions. Our fears unearth our areas of mistrust, the places where we have divorced God's sovereignty and goodness from our real situations.

Trusting the will of God is one of the most "unsafe" actions there is. And the false self's will is, by its very nature, at odds with God's will. Some of the things that God asks us to do take us out of our comfort zones and push the boundaries of our trust. And here is a frightening truth: When we are not convinced in our hearts of the utter goodness and dependability of God, when we are unable to live in the unself-conscious trust of the average sparrow, it becomes necessary for us to spiritualize the choices of our own will. We declare the will of the false self to be the will of God. In doing so, we might lead comfortable lives with safe professions, secure neighborhoods, and insulated routines and relationships, but we will never understand the true heartbeat of Jesus. We will never answer his call to live a life abandoned to him, a life that is at once huge and heroic.

The Trap of Created Love

For as long as she could remember, Anna craved esteem, affirmation, and the approval of others. Her father drank too much and was emotionally unavailable to her. To attract the love she craved, Anna became a chameleon, adapting herself to what everyone else wanted her to be. The drive to attain love ruled her life: "I always had to be doing all these things to make sure I was the apple of someone's eye. If I wasn't, it was scary. I just wanted to do what would make everyone else the happiest with me." When Anna received the external affirmation she desired, however, she still felt a huge emptiness inside. She experienced no freedom in that kind of esteem. These days, Anna is learning to receive the love of God in life-changing ways, but she can still recall how furious the drive for affirmation once was: "Approval is an addiction. You can't ever get enough of it, and you can't find a sense of self. You're an empty pit desperately longing for someone to tell you who you are."

We all enjoy a pat on the back, an expression of appreciation for a job well done. Perhaps we choose service that is highly visible so that others will be grateful and like us more. Maybe they'll even love us—that's what we truly desire. But the word *esteem* is more accurate than the word *love,* because what the old self craves is external experiences of respect, affection, and approval. These things, however, merely add paint to mask, having nothing to do with authentic love.

But what happens when we don't receive such affirmations? We might experience an emptiness and, like Anna, find ourselves scratching and scrapping to be noticed, to gain for ourselves that much-prized attention. In such a situation, the false self is in residence, and what the false self wants is to be validated, to be a worthwhile person, independent of God. But because the false self refuses God's *agape* love, its demands will never be satiated. Feeding this false self is like drinking salt water to quench a burning thirst.

We were created to receive love, and if we reject the love of God, we must seek it elsewhere. The false self desires a kind of obvious and external love and esteem but only from its environment. The vague, counterfeit "love" it chases is designed to reinforce its unreality, not to provide true transformation. The false self must seal itself off from the love of God, because receiving God's love would melt this self like wax in a flame. To the false self, God's love is threatening, because it is a gift that cannot be won through performance. And if the false self

receives what it did not generate, it must admit that it lacks the
control and the goodness required to earn the prize. Receiving
real love automatically changes our self-definition, and all that
holds the false self together is a list of fragile definitions.

Some time ago while spending a few days on a personal prayer
retreat, I came to see—again and deeper—how large is the unreal persona I had created. Amidst a snowy and frigid November, I basked in the amber glow of a cabin's pine walls—reading,
writing, praying. I journaled a great deal on that retreat, lost in
excitement about the insights that leapt from my pen. In an
unconscious way, I was justifying the decision to take the retreat by the caliber of my thoughts, letting those ideas make
me feel more lovable in God's sight. During an instance of
clarity, my unhealthy need for validation skimmed the surface
of my consciousness. I heard God say, in unusually clear terms,
"You take my gifts and turn them into trophies."

It was true. Instead of holding insights as simple gifts, I turned
them into badges of my worthiness or importance. I used them
as evidence that God and others should shower me with applause and attention. My little spiritual triumphs were offered
to others like hors d'oeuvres on a plate. In doing so, the original gift was profaned while the false self received the one vote
necessary to maintain its hold. My behavior was a way to ask
God and my community, over and over, the old questions: "Do
you esteem me?" or "Am I worthy of your attention now?"

I prefer to be liked; most people would say the same. And
there's nothing wrong with wanting to be loved, and in fact,
the love of God needs to define our personhood. The trap is
sprung when that legitimate desire is usurped and replaced by
a life shaped to constantly receive human responses of esteem.
And we funnel that esteem into the place that was originally
designed to overflow with the love of God. We want people
rather than God to fill us.

Think about your life. How important is it that you find
yourself buoyed by accolades, respect, and affection? Does your
inner life rise and fall by the amount of tangible expressions of

love you receive from others? Is it possible for the positive things you do to ever remain anonymous? Do you willingly embrace the hidden, toilet-scrubbing tasks of life, or do you have to always be the star, the one in the limelight?

This need for even small forms of stardom is especially repugnant in those who minister. We appear to serve God but bow down to the drive for esteem that perpetuates the false self. I've witnessed workers who received much attention for their selfless ministry feats, while at the same time neglecting their families, jobs, or other acts of kindness because these activities garnered less recognition and strokes. In Galatians, Paul makes it clear that we can't have it both ways: "Am I now trying to win the approval of men, or of God? Or am I still trying to please men? If I were still trying to please men, I would not be a servant of Christ" (1:10).

What kind of love do you allow to fill your core? You have choices. One is to receive the love of God, which has no beginning and no end, a love that originates in God and is, therefore, uncreated.

If I'm unwilling to accept God's abundant and uncreated love, the only other choice is conditional love, love that I believe I've created and caused to exist through my behaviors. The price of this created love is an unending need to be fed human expressions of esteem because my lovability is far from a settled issue. Souls impoverished by such a stance wander in the far country, attempting to grasp in the human arena what can only be humbly received from God.

The Peril of Power

The last of the false-self drives, that of power, may be the most damaging. Everyone reading this paragraph has at some time been wounded, devastated even, by someone's drive for power. In both church and marketplace, the pursuit of power is the norm. The primary difference is that within the church, its presence tends to be more covert, camouflaged by a superficial veneer of godliness. Our faith communities are so drenched by the pursuit of power that we are more likely to notice its absence than its presence. Little qualitative difference can, in fact, be delineated between Christian and secular culture's relationship to power or how often it's used as a means to some self-centered end.

The primary difference between the false and true self can be best rendered in relation to power: one is concerned with the love of power, and the other is concerned with the power of love. And for the false self, what is the nature of that power? One word: control.

Since the false self is all shadow and no substance, it must carefully arrange its environment to maintain the illusion of power. This behavior is fleshed out through the control of people and circumstances in order to maintain a sense of well-being and to convince the world of the false self's reality. The false self enjoys and, in fact, needs to feel in charge of its surroundings. Often this drive for control works itself out in subtle ways through shaming and manipulation cloaked in apparent virtue or Christian concern. Because the false self is completely centered on surface behaviors, it must take great care to create an environment in which its power base is secure and its vision of itself untarnished.

Some years ago I was peripherally involved with a church plant pastored by Jim, a close friend. Its members consisted primarily of folks who had been wounded by another church, and they called Jim to lead the new fellowship. The core group was openly affectionate, eager to do good, and made up of tireless workers. They were bright, upper-middle-class people, typical by all appearances. Things went well—for a while.

I noticed these people attempted to buddy up with Jim, to align themselves with him, to seek roles on the church council, and to direct the weekly services. In the early days, Jim could do no wrong. Once a routine was established, my friend began to discern with God the church's direction. Some disagreed. He also refused to become everyone's closest friend. Others were angered. Slanderous whisperings about Jim's leadership ensued. Charges of false shepherding shot through church meetings. Backbiting became common.

In time, once the fruit became evident, the nature of the self that these folks embraced was undeniable. Many in the congregation started the church not to serve others but to be in control. Key leaders befriended Jim not out of love but to rule through him or to gain power by association. And when their power base was threatened, when things didn't go their way, they retaliated. Dissension drenched the fledgling congregation. Recalling that time, Jim says, "I always thought power was obvious. I learned that Christians' use of power is very oblique, syrupy sweet, and very toxic. If it were obvious, we'd all be repulsed by it and label it as un-Christian. But we cloak it in false graces and it's deadly on the inside." After nine months of in-the-name-of-Jesus behavior that would have made pagans blush, the church disbanded, and my friend was left crushed.

Perhaps this story sounds extreme. It's not. In ways that are both sly and subtle, small and large, this kind of behavior plays itself out within our churches every day. Much of the service and ministry done in our churches today is brokered by the false self, often specifically guided by its drive for power. We jockey for position within committee meetings to get our way, we do ministry to be able to control things, we have conversations in the foyer to convince others that our ideas are superior. With a Christian smile pasted on our faces, we use power to get what we want, to maintain a sense of comfort and control—all to fortify a self God can't even recognize. Jim talks about how hard it is to pinpoint false-self power in Christian circles: "The overarching thing is how successfully the power can be masked by a pseudospirituality that you don't know is pseudo. It's not confrontable because it invokes the name of God—'God spoke to me . . . ,' 'I felt led by God. . . . ' The name of God is used to endorse the behavior." Henri Nouwen states the danger bluntly: "The most insidious, divisive, and wounding power is the power used in the service of God."[7] But, of course, we're not serving God. Instead, we abuse the name of our precious Lord Jesus to bow down to the god of our own power. And what we do can look so good to the casual observer that we're even deluded into thinking God doesn't see what's really going on. But God most certainly does see, it does matter—and he is not fooled.

Power brokering is not new. The temptations of a life ruled by the false self's drive for power have been present since the dawn of human consciousness. Satan encouraged Adam and Eve to eat of the tree of the knowledge of good and evil in the Garden, saying, "God knows that when you eat of it your eyes will be opened, and you will be like God, knowing good and evil" (Gen. 3:4). What Satan offered to them was, among other things, a false identity—eat and you will become godlike since you will know good and evil as God does.

As their hands reached toward that fateful fruit, the false self—a sin self—was born. After partaking of the fruit, Adam and Eve realized their nakedness and hid from God's presence. God called, "Where are you?" (v. 9), a question surely recognizing the shift in their spiritual location, where they could no longer abide in God's presence. In the same way, when we ingest the false and forbidden fruit of power, our spiritual location instantly shifts, and we have separated ourselves from God. For Adam and Eve, the wearing of fig leaves began, and we've been to covering up with the false self ever since.

Consider the story from a slightly different angle, removing our preconceived judgments about Adam and Eve's action. The fruit was eaten out of a desire to be like God; this was the serpent's promise. Generally speaking, this desire has the semblance of goodness about it. Who among the faithful flock would not say that becoming Christlike is a goal of the Christian life? Aside from the obvious reason of disobedience to God's command, why did Adam and Eve's attempt to become like God break rather than promote relationship? Why do our own attempts to pursue godliness sometimes seem to further alienate us from the God we say we want to serve?

Like us, Adam and Eve wanted to accomplish their quest for godliness through the garnering of power rather than love. Satan pushed godlikeness under their noses, but it was not founded in a desire to become like God through love and obedience. The temptation was to grab for themselves godlikeness through rivaling God in knowledge, itself a great source of power.

This desire may appear good, at least for a season. That's why the false self can be so insidious; it often appears virtuous. But imitating Adam and Eve's motivation produces action that seeks to look godly without actually having to be godly. It's a motivation born of power, not love; therefore, while its colors appear life-giving, the fruit brings death and destruction. This is always the result of false-self power exercised within the church, and the number of people wounded by such encounters is staggering. Ephesians instructs us to, in contrast, "put on the new self, *created to be like God in true righteousness and holiness*" (4:24, italics added) where God-likeness emerges from embracing the pure will of the Lord.

What motivates you in your work and your relationships? How often do you give in to one-upmanship or the need to put people "in their places" through words and action? What propels you into ministry? Is it a desire to control people or manipulate situations? Do you tend to seek after the positions that contain maximum influence? Do you gladly engage in invisible acts of kindness that possess no chance of promoting your position or reputation, ministry so hidden you barely acknowledge it standing alone before your Lord? If you seek to live as Jesus did, you must take the path that Jesus took of relinquishing control, the path of constant submission to God, the way of powerlessness.

In the final analysis, there are two motivations for all spiritual action—love and power (the definition of power here is broadened to include any self-centered, ego-driven payoff sought in our actions). Every change affected in faith communities—and human affairs as a whole—derives from one of these two sources of motivation: we act to either give or receive the authentic love of God, or we play the false self's power game while parading in a sheepskin of Christian love. The two motivations are mutually exclusive. We are called most insistently by Jesus to love each other, and if we refuse this call or have no godly love to give, we will seek action founded in false-self power. While our motives are always mixed, either power or love will anchor and generate the primary energy for all of our behaviors. Although these behaviors may appear identical, the deed birthed from power has no meaning in the economy of God and contains nothing of eternal value.

We who must live daily with the allure of power as the foundation of our activities do well to remember Jesus' warning: "Many will say to me on that day, 'Lord, Lord, did we not prophesy in your name, and in your name drive out demons and perform many miracles?' Then I will tell them plainly, 'I never knew you. Away from me, you evildoers'" (Matt. 7:22–23). Does Jesus' declaration stir anything in your spirit? The individuals in this Scripture did seemingly right behaviors—these were all deeds Jesus himself did—yet Jesus called them doers of evil. Obviously, the key issue is not the actions but the heart behind them. Can you pause and listen for God to tell you which areas of your life are motivated by power—because they surely exist. As this Scripture points out, whether we're handing out bulletins or leading stadiums full of people to Christ, *why* we do what we do is of paramount importance. Motives matter. Everything birthed of power is a decisive "no" to God, and we ourselves are in spiritual peril. Only that which is done in and through God's love is ultimately recognized, is meaningful, and will survive the fires of eternity.

Choosing God

Everyone of us possesses a false or old self. It's standard equipment as human beings in a fallen world. As long as we are in engaged in human relationships, the temptation will remain to forsake the self that God created and exile ourselves from the Eden of our real self. But we can recognize the impostor and cut short its residency. Doing so is no small matter.

It is impossible to plumb the depths of Jesus Christ without at least an implicit theology of the old or false self. In Matthew 4, Jesus is led into the wilderness for forty days. Jesus' earthly ministry has not yet begun, and the Devil seizes upon what is really his last ripe opportunity to derail the kingdom of God. And what does the tempter dangle in front of Jesus in this last-ditch attempt to gain the cosmic upper hand? The sinful drives of the false self. Satan appeals to Jesus' hunger: "Change these stones into bread and feed yourself." Jesus responds to this demonic temptation of physical security by embracing the only true source of security: "Man does not live on bread alone, but on every word that comes from the mouth of God" (Matt. 4:4).

Satan then tosses out the false-self bait of esteem; he goads Jesus to jump from the highest point of the temple in Jerusalem and be caught in a net of angels. Why the temple and not just a high mountain? Because through this spectacular display, everyone—Jesus' enemies and friends alike—would have to marvel and proclaim that Jesus really is the Son of God. Jesus knows that to embrace this kind of esteem is to "put the Lord your God to the test" (Matt. 4:7).

The Devil saves until last the most obvious temptation—power and control. He unfurls the glitter of all this world's kingdoms, offering it all for Jesus to rule if he will bow down. Eternally steadfast, Jesus triumphs in this last temptation: "Away from me, Satan! For it is written: 'Worship the Lord your God, and serve him only'" (Matt. 4:10).

And that's the whole point in understanding and guarding ourselves against the false self: that we might worship God alone and serve him with undivided and unfettered hearts.

Whom do you worship, not with your mouth but, deeper, with your motives? The false-self drives that Satan used to tempt Jesus were designed to prod him into worshiping another. When we succumb to letting our actions, our service, be rooted in garnering outward emblems of security, esteem, and power, then we are certainly not worshiping God. But we must go further and admit the hard thing: that these drives are subtle but very real ways of worshiping the ways of Satan.

The moment of your temptation in the wilderness of this fallen world is now. And the decision you make is pivotal because, as was true for Jesus, your choice will determine whom you worship. But because Jesus emerged in perfect triumph from his false-self temptations, there is great hope for you and for us all. God is calling us to come back, to choose him, and to forsake the drives of the old self.

What is God saying to you right now about the false self? Can you understand and confess the ways that the drives of power, esteem, and security have diverted your real journey and have counterfeited within you the authentic life of God? Paul reminds us, "It is for freedom that Christ has set us free" (Gal. 5:1). Are you ready for life, not just rumors of life?

But the obstacles remain many, the pitfalls still precarious. Understanding the false-self cycle arms us with potent tools, but in order to fully move past godless culture into God encounter, we must dig deeper. We must, even in the face of fear, anxiety, and desolateness, thoroughly confront the old, false self. We must explore the depths of false-self identity and idolatry and allow God to awaken us to the ways of the true self. In consenting to this journey, we choose life, choose reality, and, ultimately, choose the God apart from whom we can do nothing.

4

WOUNDED SHADOWS

Our False-Self Identities

*The prayer preceding all prayers is "May it be the real I who
speaks. May it be the real Thou that I speak to."*
—*C. S. Lewis*

*I have been crucified with Christ and I no longer live, but
Christ lives in me. The life I live in the body, I live by faith in
the Son of God, who loved me and gave himself for me. I do not
set aside the grace of God, for if righteousness could be gained
through the law, Christ died for nothing!*
—*Paul (Galatians 2:20–21)*

entoring is a hard business. That was my thought as I mo-
tored down 35W toward home one evening. Especially spiritual mentoring. Beyond all teaching and prayer and modeling,
there's a place inside the soul, an innermost court, a holy of
holies, where none but God can go. While I knew this, I still
felt like a dismal failure as a spiritual guide and began to dis-
sect the night's events.

The topic was grace—God's unconditional and unmerited
favor freely bestowed upon us, the objects of his affection. But

that night the small group discussion digressed from observations on the assigned chapter. Only two of the members were able to meet, and in that smaller context, they felt safe to open up about their feelings about God and themselves.

One young woman had been raised in an evangelical church her whole life, and the other came to Christ as a teenager. Both had attended a Christian college and were active in church life. I had spiritually invested in these young women, pouring out hours of time, both individually and in groups. Yet it became clear, in the pure light of honesty that June evening, that in spite of all the Christian teaching and intensive discipleship each had received, both women harbored a negative self-concept and possessed images of God that were threatening to them. Because of these strongly held ideas, they experienced little love or joy in their Christian walk.

It had all been spilled out on the table: fear alternating with apathy toward God, guilt over not having devotions, guilt over not feeling enough guilt, all wrapped up in self-disappointment and self-loathing. I was grateful for their honesty, and we prayed for Jesus to step into their struggle. But I was left frustrated and somber on the drive home. I agonized over what I couldn't touch, over my inability to adequately communicate the deeper things of God. But mostly I mourned the possibility that these young women might never truly embrace and experience God's goodness.

What scared me was how much they knew. Few Christians possessed the amount of biblical knowledge they had. And they were exposed to the real deal about grace. *If they can't "get it,"* I thought, *then who can?* But the problem wasn't about what they knew—theologically they were perfectly sound—but about something much less tangible. Amid accurate presentations of truth and authentic models of relationship with God, something was still askew. False images and ideas led these women around by their spiritual noses. The false self's ways infected their spirituality from within and without.

These young women were not alone in their struggle. Their

dilemma is the sad secret of believers everywhere—that even after years of spiritual teaching and discipleship, there exists for most Christians a vague dislike of self and a nagging fear of God.

Henry David Thoreau said that a thousand hack at the branches of evil for every one who strikes at the root. When we talk about the false self, what is the root, the place of confrontation and transformation? The bedrock, the very root, of the false self is twofold. First, is a degraded identity, the erroneous way we see ourselves; second, is idolatry, the erroneous way we view God. The two are inseparable.

False Self, False God

The false self's drive for earthly emblems of power, security, and esteem jeopardize the spiritual life of those who desire to follow Christ. But the false self is much more than behaviors that divide us from godliness. Much of the advice we receive from spiritual guides in evangelical circles, however, boils down to changing behaviors. This approach often has us, in essence, trading in the false self for a newer model that looks better or acts nicer. If we focus only upon fixing our actions, we are no less lost than before; we just *appear* to be less lost.

Authentic change must occur at a far deeper level. The false self is not merely a peripheral nuisance or spiritual inconvenience. The stakes are much higher because the false-self system culminates in idolatry. When the false self is embraced as our identity, someone or something other than God tells us who we are at our core. Thus, whatever we allow to define our personhood is an object of our worship since identity is so foundational to the spiritual life. Think about it: how can the false self justify its behaviors and maintain its illusory sense of reality while worshiping the true God? It can't. It must distance itself from God, but if this false self claims Christian allegiance, then it must pray to *somebody;* it must worship *something.* Indeed, it does pray, and it does worship—but not the true God.

What do we worship when we are in the false self? In Luke 18, Jesus' story of the Pharisee and the tax collector distinguishes true people of prayer from pretenders. The tax collector prayed for mercy to a loving God while the Pharisee went to the temple and "prayed about himself" (v. 11). The preposition *about* can also be rendered *to,* meaning the Pharisee was praying to himself about his good works as if he himself were the intended recipient of his prayer, his own deity. The false self creates a false god. The christianized false self must worship an idol, or it couldn't exist. A version of God is created that reflects and reinforces the false self's vision of itself.

This idolatry is not prevented or corrected by right theological ideas about God alone. Like the young women I mentored, many Christians have accurate intellectual pictures of who God is, yet have difficulty actualizing that truth in everyday, functional interactions with God. The truth is, revelation needs to be accompanied by transformation. And, again, to receive God's transformation, it is necessary to understand the schism between head and heart—we cognitively know of God's wondrous, loving characteristics, but the God we respond to in our actual relating is radically different.

Why is healing the schism so difficult? The blueprint looks fairly simple: we take our correct ideas about God and let them become the basis of our everyday actions. But it's not that easy. Vision of self and vision of God are inextricably tied together. Who we say God is says a lot about who we believe we are, and conversely, who we say we are speaks loudly of how we view God. In order to confront our skewed ideas about God, we must face the erroneous but comfortable ideas that we cling to for our identity. To see God for who he truly is, not just in ideas but in actual living, requires a dramatic shift—again, a *metanoia*—in how we perceive and understand life.

Turning from idolatry is the key to the journey of transformation. And to begin this part of the journey, we must understand how God becomes dethroned.

Transference and Idolatry

Dethroned? I recall an old gospel tract that contained line drawings of "me," God, and throne chairs. The stick person that's me used to be on that throne, but I bent my knee to Jesus, and now the little cloud with capital G-O-D hovers on that chair in the center of my heart. Isn't that how it works?

Yes, on one level. But all of us come into the kingdom with wounds that must be reckoned with. Some of these wounds affect the way that we see God. We don't realize it, but we have put on the throne a version of God that we ourselves have helped to draw, a strange melding of the cloud and the stick person. The real God gets mixed in with ideas born of our old wounds. This type of dethroning occurs through *transference*.

Transference is a well-known psychological phenomenon that counselors and therapists encounter regularly. Transference takes a past wound and attaches its afflicted emotions and needs to a current person or situation. When a client revisits a painful memory, particularly if it involved an authority figure, the client may react to the therapist (a current authority figure) as if she or he were the perpetrator from long ago. Transference can occur even if the current situation is completely removed from the wounding event, and the therapist in the present tense is entirely unlike the person who caused the original hurt. Transference frequently erupts with differing human authority figures, but the discussion here focuses on how transference intersects our relationship with God.

The false self was created as a reaction to not being loved unconditionally and to receiving instead messages about our defectiveness and need to earn love. With no reliable foundation of *agape* love, these negative messages are internalized, defining the deep self, and then projected onto the ultimate authority figure—God. Transference takes our troubling experiences and wounded emotions—particularly those that surround family or other people who have been in any kind of "parental" role in our lives—and pastes them over the real message and person of God, thus creating an idolatrous god figure.

Say a certain father was an emotionally abusive parent who eventually ran out on the family. His son Jerry carries the wounds caused by the father, but he manages to grow up and copes as best he can. Jerry finds a vibrant church led by caring, charismatic Pastor Mike, who takes an interest in Jerry's spiritual development. Jerry is thrilled and flattered and begins his discipleship with Mike.

But problems soon arise. Jerry suddenly finds himself living more and more in fear concerning the relationship. What if he's late for an appointment with the pastor? What if he says the wrong thing? He harbors images of Mike becoming angry and lashing out. Jerry finds himself walking on eggshells although the pastor's actions have provided no justification for his fears. No matter how stable and affirming Mike is, Jerry struggles deeply with trusting his loving elder. He also is fearful that his mentor may unexpectedly sever the relationship, even though Mike has pledged to walk by him. Jerry has transferred his wounded feelings about his father onto Pastor Mike, and as a result of this transference, Jerry is relating to Mike as if he were his father.

When interacting with humans, we can readily observe those actions which contradict the fears born of woundedness that fuel transference. But in the faith arena, we relate to a God who is spirit and who possesses a different type of tangibility. Thus, it is easier to misread and misperceive God, so transference can continue unabated for an entire lifetime. The result of such transference is a spiritual life shadowed by idolatry, as the image of God is traded for a substitute created by our woundedness.

The Lord reminds us, "I am God, and not man" (Hos. 11:9), and Jesus' ministry was often one of correcting our distorted views of God. Jesus assures us in Matthew 6 that God will meet our needs, so we don't have to obsessively chase after the stuff of daily life. With three similar parables, Luke 15 drives deep the message of God's unwavering concern and our personal value to him: whether we're a wandering sheep, a coin knocked into a dark, hidden place, or a disrespectful son with tainted motives, God's care is relentless, and he deeply desires our return. Jesus understood that we need help in differentiating God from other authority figures: "Which of you, if his son asks for bread, will give him a stone? Or if he asks for a fish, will give him a snake? If you, then, though you are evil, know how to give good gifts to your children, *how much more will your Father in heaven give good gifts to those who ask him!*" (Matt. 7:9–11, italics added).

Transference begins with our false and wounded self and ends with projecting our woundedness onto God, thereby creating a distortion of God. That's idolatry. To further understand the false self/false god connection, it will be helpful to examine two paradigms: the performing false self and the degraded false self.

The Performing False Self

Gina's mother was a perfectionist. In her home, in her entertaining, in her dress, in her work, everything had to be perfect. From the carpets that were vacuumed daily to the exact positioning of the expensive figurines in the curio cabinet, the world Gina grew up in provided her with a central message: life was about appearances and performance. Gina recalls the stress of her childhood: "There was a lot of rigidity to daily life. I felt I needed to know my mother's expectations before she stated them. If she had to bring one of her expectations to light, then I had failed." Gina grew up believing that her job in life was to know not only her mother's expectations but everyone's and to not just meet them but to exceed them. What mattered was Gina's taste in clothes, her grades in school, her professional titles—and how she performed in all the arenas of life. Gina's church only reinforced the focus on performance. All the families were well dressed and "together" with no visible signs—ever—of trouble.

Eventually, when the performance-driven machinery of her life ran out of gas, a tired and broken Gina entered counseling and was ministered to by gracious, godly mentors.

Like Gina, Mark grew up driven to give everything his best effort. His parents reinforced his desire to excel: "They taught me to always do things the best possible way, to be totally perfect. I was a straight 'A' student, and if I ever got an 'A-,' my dad told me I should be only getting 'As.'" As a result, Mark had to be tops at everything. Through the years, he performed well academically and was heavily involved in school, sports, and civic activities, often holding leadership roles. His activities within the church were vital once he became a Christian, and he used service to help right the scales for the sinful choices of his past. He says, "Spiritually, I thought I always needed to be doing something. It was hard for me to realize I could just sit with God. To prove my worth to God, I'd do things such as speaking at youth conventions and doing street witnessing. I was going around telling people God loved them, and I wasn't even sure if he loved me." Mark lived a constricted existence, always afraid of God, believing if he could only stockpile enough good behaviors, God might eventually love him.

Do these two stories resonate with you? We all know high achievers or overachievers, and any of us may be one. Whether it's climbing to the heights of a profession, seeking a perfect grade point average, needing to raise flawless children, or engaging in unblemished service to God, most of us have felt the drive to perform well. But for many, this drive goes beyond the desire to simply do one's work well; it is actually a compulsion, and people like Mark and Gina are not *free* to perform well but *must* perform well in order to maintain a consistent self-concept and sense of well-being. This type of disposition is a sign of the performing false self. If any type of achievement becomes a litmus test of worth or lovableness, it's an indication that the performing false self is in residence.

And the word *achievement* must be understood very broadly. Good performance needn't be obviously competitive. Anything that is earnestly sought in order to reinforce identity becomes a function of the performing false self. Earlier in my life, my goal was to achieve success in relationships, to live under and be defined by the banner "Good Friend." Maintaining relationships through tireless listening and through rivaling Dear Abby in my sage advice was a major form of achievement. It had the appearance of goodness and selflessness and allowed me to say a hearty "tsk, tsk" to those who seemed caught up in more "worldly" performance goals. But if the basis of my friendships is to secure a sense of well-being and bolster a false identity, then I am no better than the most ravenous corporate raider.

The performing false self clearly hears the harsh and untrue messages from authority figures, and its response is to do better, try harder, seek a level of perfection that will disprove, or at least cover up, its defectiveness. This self wants to earn love and affection. The path of the performing false self can be seen in the following diagram:

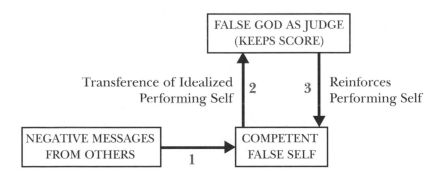

In this diagram, the negative messages are absorbed into the deep self. Once this unaffirming vision is internalized, a competent false self is created. This mask declares to the world that the false self is worthy of love and esteem. As Gina's and Mark's stories demonstrate, the source of such a person's worth is achievement, not God, which creates a need to engage in a continuous race for acclaim and applause.

Because the achievement focus of the competent self is projected into its vision of God, the first arrow above the competent false-self box points up toward a false god. Transference is at work here: a biblical deity, heavily revised by the negative messages, is now on the throne. For the competent false self, God is seen as Judge and Chief Scorekeeper. This god sits on the sidelines, applauding the accomplishments of the ever-active, always striving believer. And the values of the performing false self must match the values held by this god in order to justify the competitive behaviors linked to earthly successes.

Gina readily admits that in her performing false self she transferred her negative feelings about herself onto a scorekeeping god: "When I performed well, I felt God was incredibly pleased with me. When I failed at something, that was about my being a failure, and God saw me as a failure. My own sense of failure and shame was transferred onto him. I was not able to differentiate my views of myself and God's view of me. They were one and the same." Mark echoes Gina's impression that God's love for him could vary greatly, and God's approval was based upon his performance: "When I wasn't the best, I felt like God wouldn't look at me. I felt that rather than asking him for help, I needed to get better first, then I could go to him. I thought he saw me as flawed, unworthy, unlovable."

The false god that is worshiped in such cases is actually an idealized version of the competent self. The false god reinforces the performing self with feedback based on how well the false self performs in the world, this feedback being represented by the second arrow that points down to the competent false self. The false god reacts to, and its disposition is always gauged by, the believer's actions. There is no consistent regard for the performer. Good performance garners well-earned praise and positive reinforcement; poor performance is met with shame and the message to try harder next time.

Shame. That's one of the primary results of the performing false-self system. Shame spotlights the believer's most dreaded fears about his or her defectiveness, exposing them like an open wound. Shame and performance are closely tied together as Gina so wisely observes: "The root of performance is shame. The need to perform is actually a defense against shame. When I start being shamed by my mother for not performing well, my automatic defense is to do everything possible to make her disappointment not happen again." Fear of shame keeps the performer in a frantic dance. But when performance falters, as it must, the believer is steeped in a core sense of defectiveness and unworthiness that secretly guides the performer's life— spiritual and otherwise.

So what must the performing false self do in the face of such potent shame? Keep performing. There are no other options. Because good performance is so monumentally important, the performing false self *is* what it is able to *achieve* and, conversely, achievement completely defines this self. Mark got so caught up in the achievements within his activities that they eventually defined him. He sums up his performance-based outlook: "The way that I grew up said that what you do is so important that it becomes who you are." When we become entangled within this way of life, a sense of self comes only from how well we perform. Our lives become fed and ruled by measurable externals, such as approval of significant others and all forms of achievement, including spiritual conquests.

Because achievement defines the performing false self, and because nonactivity is achievement-less, the person trapped in the performing false self must be in perpetual motion toward the next goal. Taking time for listening, receiving, and being— even at the feet of the Lord as did Mary—is to cease activity, to stop being whom we think we are and, therefore, to enter non-existence. Both Mark and Gina experienced a real dread around stopping the hamster wheel of performance. Mark says that letting go of his relentless search for measurable perfection meant "facing the anxiety and fear that I'd never be lovable to anyone, including God." To avoid such fear and anxiety, he had to keep performing, keep achieving, even when he felt trapped by it. When we're ensnared in the performing false self, we become compulsively busy, finding it difficult, if not impossible, to embrace times of rest, reflection, and quiet, not only because such times lack a prize but also because they uncover feelings of self-loathing that ultimately fuel the race.

And while caught in the performing false self, we must never admit our needs. A denial of human neediness is a hallmark of the performing false self. Generally speaking, legalism itself is, in fact, fueled by despising legitimate needs and human weaknesses. When functioning in this paradigm and asked what we need, we typically stare or give a superficial answer: "I need my aunt's surgery to go well," or "I need to get a job promotion I applied for." If we do give a more personal answer, it's generally about God giving us strength to keep performing well, to keep striving after all our performance-based goals.

But as the performer, we are completely exiled from our inner lives, that which is deeply necessary and true about ourselves. And while we may from time to time sense the heart's needs, to respond would be to knock out one of the pillars that supports the false self—the idea that we have no needs or that to dwell on them is selfish.

As a result, for the performing false self, the head-centered, intellectual posture becomes the sole path of relationship with God, since the heart-centered posture disrupts self-definition. The head/heart split must remain intact in order for the performing false self to keep working. In order to validate the performer's idolatrous pursuits, the heart-centered posture is forsaken, even feared or labeled as evil.

The Pharisees who crowded around Jesus present a classic picture of the performing false self. They were so entangled in, and identified with, rules and outward symbols of holy achievement that God's presence presented a deadly contradiction. The god they imaged and served well was as condemning, superficial, and nitpicky as they, and Jesus openly confronted their focus on external achievement. The parable alluded to earlier, that of the Pharisee and the tax collector, is a potent picture of the performing false self:

To some who were confident of their own righteousness and looked down on everybody else, Jesus told this parable: "Two men went up to the temple to pray, one a Pharisee and the other a tax collector. The Pharisee stood up and prayed about himself: 'God, I thank you that I am not like other men—robbers, evildoers, adulterers—or even like this tax collector. I fast twice a week and give a tenth of all I get.' But the tax collector stood at a distance. He would not even look up to heaven, but beat his breast and said, 'God, have mercy on me, a sinner.' I tell you that this man, rather than the other, went home justified before God. For everyone who exalts himself will be humbled, and he who humbles himself will be exalted." (Luke 18:9–14)

The tax collector correctly labeled both himself and his deity—a sinner appealing to a merciful God. Unlike the tax collector, the Pharisee felt secure before his god only when he performed well, and this god was a perfected version of himself. He put his "confidence in the flesh," so his identity came from spiritual performance and external comparison. Likewise, those of us caught in the performing false self become obsessed with our own brand of righteousness and with whether or not our spiritual yardstick indicates we have merited favor.

Do portions of your spiritual journey mirror the fearful and anxious existence of the performing false self? Can you identify thoughts and feelings that you hold about God and yourself that point to the performer and its god? I'm not asking you to recite the theology you learned in Sunday school. I'm asking how you actually live, how your images of God and self really function in everyday life. If you're unsure about how these ideas relate to you or if you're afraid to look deeper, quiet yourself and ask the Lord to help you to examine the ways that the performing false self has marked your story. Without facing the truth about the false self that has driven your life and about the false god it worships, you won't be able to deeply receive your God-created true self.

The Degraded Self

To one degree or another, the performing false self has influenced the sense of self and of God for almost all of us. But those of us who do not strongly identify with the performer likely will recognize themselves in the degraded false self.

Catherine's parents divorced when she was three years old. The trauma to the parents—especially to her mother, who then needed to be trained for a moneymaking career—made them emotionally and physically unavailable to Catherine at critical points in her life. At school Catherine was shy and had trouble fitting in. "When I was a child, I hated myself," Catherine remembers. "I thought, 'Catherine is ugly, unlikable, unlovable, inadequate, and a disappointment.' I didn't feel like I could please people, so I really didn't try. I thought people could tell how defective I was." The self-hatred that Catherine harbored toward herself was projected onto all those around her. Today, Catherine still sometimes struggles with those early messages, but she's learning more about—and receiving in life-transforming ways—the healing love of God.

Both the performing and the degraded false selves are reactions to unaffirming voices that inevitably flow to us in a fallen world. They are two sides of the same coin. The performer's response is to prove the voices wrong; the degraded self determines to prove the voices right. Performers will cycle into the degraded false self when stricken with failed performance but only long enough to gain a second wind. Once the performer starts to tally up a new batch of good works, the sense of defectiveness will again be cloaked in performance. Rather than attempting to escape these messages, as the performer strives to do, the degraded false self is steeped in them, accepting irredeemable defectiveness as the core truth of the person. This perception of defectiveness is projected onto God—transference occurs—creating a different version of the judging god of the performer.

In my mid-twenties, when the wheels fell off my performing false self and I was left with a terrifying sense of poverty and nothingness, I cycled into an extended period where the degraded self was in residence. I felt completely defective and tumbled headlong into depression. I saw a counselor, and early on she gave me an assignment—to take a personal inventory, listing in one column on a piece of paper the things that I liked about myself and in the other column the things that I didn't like about myself. I struggled mightily with the task, lost in self-loathing and weakness. She said that the two sides needed to be fairly equal in length, so my list never got beyond four items because I could think of so few good qualities about myself (and, really, I only made it to four by cheating).

In times of extreme self-hatred—either then and or the occasional attacks now—I'm not alone. The degraded false self runs rampant throughout the family of faith. The degraded false self can be diagrammed as follows:

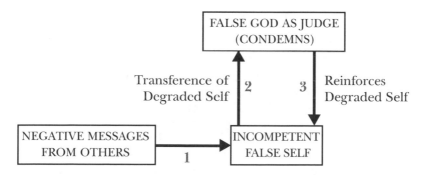

The lies of a fallen world are communicated to the degraded self and are internalized, creating a vision of the self as incompetent—defective, useless, bad. This vision creates in turn an incompetent false self whose degraded sense of self is projected onto a condemning god, who consistently affirms the degraded self's irredeemable defectiveness. In such a transference, the degraded false self pictures a god waiting to send in the lightning bolts, whose gavel always pounds out a verdict of "guilty!"

Catherine experienced this kind of transference. She felt unlovable and completely defective, and her degraded feelings about herself were ultimately projected upon God: "I knew I was a disappointment to God, and I had a lot of fear of him. I was afraid of the love part of Christianity not being true because I was so defective. I figured if there was an exception to the love rule, I would be it."

As Catherine's experience points out, this false god is a perfected version of the incompetent false self, since the god completely embodies the voice that condemns. As a consequence, the incompetent self receives additional messages from this human-made idol that constantly confirm the assessment of the person as nothing but a bundle of flaws and not worth anyone's, especially God's, attention.

This lens for seeing God and self puts the believer in a no-win situation. Positive reinforcement never penetrates the degraded self's walls of woundedness, which bear the name *defective*. Praise bounces off like BBs off of iron. Even if it might get in, the person has no place to shelve such foreign messages. On the other hand, when perceived failures occur for this person, those messages readily penetrate, find their way to the deep self, and are used to reinforce those walls. Failure is a way to say, "See, more proof that I'm really no good."

What is the fallout of the degraded self, its natural result, and its external motivator? Guilt. While the performer in us would certainly battle the presence of guilt, the degraded self revolves around it. As degraded believers, we often have a preoccupation with guilt. It becomes the thing to be avoided by acquiescing in conflict, by staying in the shadows, by attempting right (or at least not wrong) behaviors. Guilt becomes our main motivator of activity whether it's daily devotions, a halfhearted yes to church duties, or the element that keeps us in unhealthy relationships. Guilt can also solidify the paralysis of nonactivity, since we are sometimes too fearful to try to affect change.

Catherine remembers the guilt that pervaded in her life, saying, "I was always afraid of doing something wrong. If I was in a situation where I had to make a decision, I would fear all the options and then feel guilt afterward about what I chose. In my head, I could always find a way to accept responsibility for everything and experience guilt because of it." Godly guilt compels us, broken, to the feet of Jesus. The guilt of our degraded false self, however, is pure condemnation, sending us scurrying into dark corners away from God. In the world of the degraded false self, great care is taken to avoid the guilt that reminds us that we're sinking in the quicksand of sin and self-degradation.

One key indicator of the presence of either the degraded false self or the performing false self is self-hatred. Whether we're running the hamster wheel of performance or whipping ourselves for our innumerable defects, self-hatred is the common denominator. Some might protest, saying, "That's too strong a word. I certainly don't hate myself." But how often do we treat ourselves with small bursts of contempt, entertain scornful thoughts about ourselves, or think of our personhood with disdain? All of these are subtle but very potent forms of self-hatred.

Brennan Manning reminds us that self-hatred is an indecent luxury no disciple of Christ can afford. We understand the evils of pride, but we hesitate to label self-scorn as evil. It's easy to identify the focus on self that marks a life of pride. Less obvious, but just as destructive, self-hatred, too, keeps us obsessed with self. Pride and self-hatred are two expressions of the same wounding, and the fruit of both is an endless narcissism. All of life is seen in terms of how it puffs us up or pulls us down. A blessed and holy self-forgetfulness is impossible.

Self-hatred is so common within faith communities, as well as in secular society, that it's difficult to rouse people to take it seriously. But we must. Because it is so integral to the false-self system, self-hatred is the greatest obstacle to walking in the true self. And we cannot find escape by addressing self-hatred in all our traditional self-help ways. Bible verses, daily affirmations, and all the prayer in the world will not create any qualitative change if the issue of identity is untouched. If you do not address the false self, you will not uncover the root of self-hatred, and only a temporal, superficial change will result.

Is this a blueprint of your life? Is God drawing you to come present to the hidden beliefs of your existence, the secret fears you constantly avoid? To what extent are self-hatred and the degraded self hallmarks of your personal story? There is a road of healing. Difficult as it might be to accept, perhaps the obedience to which God calls you right now is not the completion of some holy to-do list. Rather, perhaps the call is to simply believe that what God says about you is true and to undertake with him the healing journey where that idea becomes a working, daily reality. This is the journey out of the false self.

Exodus from the False-Self System

Rachel is even now in the throes of her journey out of her false self. Raised as a performer, she was the shining star of the family, the one upon whom all hopes were fastened. She was overinvolved as a young person—captain of the volleyball team and the golf team, lead trombone in the jazz and the concert bands, president of her National Honor Society chapter. Performance was everything, and the facade worked for a long time. But as with most people whose true self is emerging, her exodus was initiated by a crisis. Physical brokenness—chronic fatigue syndrome—prevented her from keeping up the pace of the performer, and without performance, she no longer knows who she is. Rachel describes some of her days as if she's drowning and completely without hope. It's painful to watch, but no more so than watching a woman in labor, because I know, if she perseveres, what awaits her.

Whether through crisis or just a hunger for more of Christ, the exodus from the false self is the most significant spiritual journey we will ever undertake. We will, of course, continue to struggle with the false self. But our sojourn begins with a huge first step—prying away the mask, denying its authenticity. The journey can be far from easy and is itself a type of crisis for most. Thomas Merton describes the painful movement from false to true, from unreal to real, from old self to new:

> The difficult ascent from falsity toward truth is accomplished not through pleasant advances in wisdom and insight, but through the painful unlayering of levels of falsehood, untruths deeply embedded in our consciousness, lies which cling more tightly than a second skin. Only when we have descended in dread to the center of our nothingness, by His grace and His guidance can we be led by Him, in His own time, to find Him in losing ourselves. For the way to God lies through deep darkness in which all knowledge and all created wisdom and all pleasure and prudence and all human hope and human joy are defeated and annulled by the overwhelming purity of the light of the presence of God.[1]

Does this description surprise you? We might picture the move toward our true, God-given self as skipping through a lovely spring meadow, accompanied by bunnies and bluebirds. If this were the case, no one would tarry long in the false-self system. Rather, we are called to plunge headlong into death, a death against which the false self will hysterically fight. If we do not understand this, the minute things become uncomfortable, we'll likely race back to the anesthetic of the false self.

This transformation from false self to true ruthlessly confronts truths that will nullify much of what we hold dear. Leaving behind the wreckage of the false self can be marked by three phases or movements: dread, desert, and abandonment. While some true-self believers will not necessarily experience all these movements or in the manner described, many will find these concepts helpful in their process.

When the structures of the false self, the scaffolding of

superficiality and illusion, first start to collapse, we become untethered from all we thought solid and actual. None of the old ways of doing things—of making life fit, of knowing ourselves—works anymore. The primary response to this frightening free fall is dread. We begin to experience the true essence of the false self: nothingness. And this nothingness is not illusory; it is our condition apart from God. Yet terrible as it feels, the dread of our own extinguished self is exactly where we need to be. Merton supposes that a reason why our spiritual lives remain superficial and stunted is "that we never make this real, serious return to the center of our own nothingness before God. Hence we never enter into the deepest reality of our relationship with Him."[2] This dread must be faced, not escaped.

In moving away from the false self, we find ourselves off center—life is suddenly confusing, and nothing makes sense anymore. We feel removed from God, afraid that we've taken a huge step backward. It's as though we wake up, realize where we are, and believe that God is a million miles away. Ironically, the very realization of the false self's psychic distance from God brings us into closer consciousness of the Lord we want to love. While experiencing dread, though, we'll feel completely alienated from God. But we actually may never have been more aligned with God than in that uncomfortable, but essential, place.

The movement of dread gives way to desert. At this point, the alarm of our nothingness eases, we realize we're still here, and we enter the desert, where on a daily basis we begin to deal with the realizations that we encountered in our experience of dread. One hallmark of this desert experience is depression, a primary cause of which is the full emergence of self-hatred. Rachel acknowledges that self-hatred has been potent at times, saying, "I hated myself for my inability to feel God. I knew all these things in my head that are true about God, but I felt like an absolute contradiction. I had no sense of self and beat myself up for not trusting God."

In the desert, we believe we have all but left our spiritual journey. Self-loathing runs unchecked because it is no longer counterbalanced with performance, and the illusory structures that minimized self-hatred have now collapsed. But this is the beginning of authentically confronting self-hatred, as we must, in order to move toward discovering the true self.

We wander about the ruins of our previous self with no idea who we are or who God is. All we know is that what we previously spent the bulk of our energy building and believing is largely false, and we are understandably grieved. The false god that was the true north of our existence is gone, false, rubbish. In describing her desert experience, Rachel puts it this way: "It's shocking. You stare at the face of the thing you thought was true, the thing you have invested all this time and energy in, and then, all of a sudden, you see how worthless it is. You see how much of your life you've wasted. That's when God really broke me."

We might think ourselves "bad Christians" or "poor Christians" because of the alienation we feel from God. But such a sense of alienation can be the birth pangs of receiving something entirely new—God as God is, not as we make him. Spanish philosopher Don Miguel Unamuno speaks to such a crisis: "Those who believe they believe in God, but without passion in the heart, without anguish of mind, without uncertainty, without doubt, and even at times without despair, believe only in the idea of God, and not in God himself."[3]

Identity-less and unsure of who God is, we find ourselves with little or no spiritual motivation. We might be shocked at our lack of interest in spiritual disciplines, outreach, and service while understanding we can't muster the motivation or the muscle to mount the treadmill anymore. We're just plain tired—tired of our unruly emotions that now run the show and tired of groping through our days for our familiar handholds. What we don't know, and can't see, is that God is very present to us in the desert, and if we allow it, he will fashion the desert into what it needs to be: the place where the false-self system is purged. In order for this time to be ultimately fruitful, the fields of spiritual action might need to lie fallow for a while.

How we react to the desert is pivotal. We stand at a fork in the road, and one choice is to give in to despair, to stay lost in self-hatred, and to forsake our ever becoming God's beloved, the true-self identity rumored in the depths of our being. Our other option is hope. We may desperately want to return to the comfortable predictability of the false-self system, but when enough stability and energy to do so returns, we must reject that temptation and stay within the desert. The desert, strange as it may sound, is the terrain of hope. Like the children of Israel, we must press on toward a promised land, despite our compulsions to go back to Egypt. Rachel expresses the tension: "When you're walking through the desert, you think about how well everything worked before. You desperately want to walk in your true self, but you're just not there yet. You're totally in the middle. The inconsistency can be so wearisome at times."

Desert, when lived honestly, must eventually give way to something else—the threshold of the true self: abandonment. At this point, we realize we've survived the shipwreck and haven't drowned or been dashed upon the rocks. We sense God *is* in this journey, and we notice his action and, most important, our inaction. We understand that God is creating a change in us, and that it is God, not ourselves, who is sustaining us. Little tendrils of trust emerge. *Maybe,* we think, *this God really is love, not just in theory but in my life.* We're still not sure who we are, but our seed of trust somehow makes this fact bearable. A fragile hope emerges, and we come to pray, "God, I refuse Egypt, and I can't even imagine the promised land, so I give myself to you because I know I am lost, and I trust that you are good. May your will be done in my life."

At the edge of my own moment of abandonment, I recall experiencing an odd calmness. Like the words of an old Janis Joplin song, "Freedom's just another word for nothing left to lose," enough had been dismantled internally that I did feel strangely freed. That time was like the aftermath of a violent rainstorm. The landscape had been rearranged by its fury, but there was also a freshness and a beauty, and surprisingly, some-

thing had been nurtured by all that rain. I was ready for whatever God wanted, because my ways had taken me so far astray.
Jeanne Guyon, a Christian from the seventeenth century, says,
"Abandonment is, in fact, *the key* to the *inner court*—the key to
the fathomless depths. Abandonment is the key to the inward
spiritual life."[4]

The moment of abandonment is a movement from—to use
Gerald May's terms—willfulness to willingness. May explains the
difference between these two concepts: "Willfulness is the setting of oneself apart from the fundamental essence of life in an
attempt to master, direct, control, or otherwise manipulate existence. More simply, willingness is saying yes to the mystery of
being alive in each moment."[5] The false self spends its existence attempting to willfully control itself and God. Our time in
dread and desert softens us, reminding us that we are neither
the masters of our fates nor the captains of our souls. Willingness opens us up to cooperating with God in the formation of
a life that, we sense, will be bigger and more magnificent than
what we by ourselves could ever construct.

The temptation to exchange our true identity for a false one
is the greatest temptation that Satan will ever offer; nothing so
thoroughly dismantles our participation in the kingdom of God
than becoming a resident of that kingdom in name only. In
offering to Jesus the first two temptations—to turn stone into
bread and to throw himself from the highest point of the
temple—Satan preceded each with the phrase, "If you are the
Son of God" (Matt. 4:3, 6). Satan tried to shake Jesus loose
from his unbroken communion with the Father by tempting
Jesus to question his most basic sense of self. If Jesus had ques-
tioned his own identity by agreeing to prove who he was, he
would have ultimately served Satan. We have inherited the very
same demonic temptation to question our identification with
Christ as the source of self and to worship a lie created by the
Father of Lies.

Central to Jesus' message was the truth about who God is
and who we are; both are of ultimate importance in the spiritual

life. Brennan Manning says that if our image of God becomes
healed, the image we hold of ourselves will likewise be healed.
And if we discover our true self, we will also find God. The
search for the true self and the search for God are the same
journey in that our true self is bound up with encountering
the person of Jesus Christ.

We *can* quit dancing around, trying to earn love and a sense
of identity from things that are not capable of giving them.

Are you willing to forsake the false self and the idol it worships? Are you prepared to begin the journey? Are you ready
to come home? Too much time has been squandered in the far
country of ghosts and shadows. And that's all that these selves
and gods are—phantoms without substance or strength, possessing no reality except that which you give them.

Perhaps you've always resisted taking that first step, maybe
without knowing why, but the time has come to firmly point
your feet toward the house of the Father.

5

ULTIMATE IDENTITY
AND TRUE-SELF RELATING

*I tell you the truth, unless a kernel of wheat falls to the ground
and dies, it remains only a single seed. But if it dies, it produces
many seeds. The man who loves his life will lose it, while the
man who hates his life in this world will keep it for eternal life.
Whoever serves me must follow me; and where I am, my
servant also will be.*
—Jesus (John 12:24–26)

*How can we die to the false self, if it is the only self we know?
If we die to the false self and we do not know the true self,
where are we?*
—Basil Pennington

He must become greater; I must become less.
—John the Baptist (John 3:30)

𝒥magine a huge, ornate room—beautiful and sumptuous with
colors, fabrics, polished wood. You're sitting at a long table

laden with every culinary delicacy ever created. The candles
are lit, many guests who know and love you are present, and
happy music reverberates from every corner. Jesus himself is
the host of the gathering. The realization comes slowly, and
in great astonishment it hits you: It's a party in your honor.
Jesus stands, clears his throat, and with his eyes fixed upon
you, proclaims with great delight to all present, "You have
stolen my heart with one glance of your eyes. How delightful
is your love. . . . Arise, come my darling, my beautiful one,
come with me." And above your head is a huge sign that
stretches twenty feet in length emblazoned with the words "I
love . . ." followed by a name—your name! Overwhelmed, your
joy in Jesus, your Beloved, resonates with praise, and you cry
out, "My lover is mine and I am his!" You've never been more
at home or more alive than in this room at this moment.
Within that sacred place, love is the very air you breathe. Can
you see it—even a little? If you can, you have a pictorial primer
on the life of the true self—a picture taken from the Song of
Solomon: "He has taken me to the banquet hall, and his banner over me is love" (2:4).[1]

But the truth depicted in this scene is not mere imagination.
It is the proper state of the human soul in Christ, what is most
real about your life and mine. Thomas Merton says, "There is
no true spiritual life outside the love of Christ. We have a spiritual life only because we are loved by Him."[2] This love that
watches sparrows, that embraces wayward lambs, that spoke
into being all that is—this love is the essence of our true self.
Remove your shoes, for the ground we are about to walk upon
is holy. When talking about the true self, we open to something that is very tender, and that which is most precious and
intimate about God and about ourselves is touched.

Our thoughts and imaginings around the true self, however,
are woefully impoverished, even skewed and corrupt. The theology relative to the true self is usually attached to outward
behaviors and roles while the core is rarely taught or proclaimed.
Yet the true self will exist for all eternity, and it is for this self

that Jesus died. Thus, we can do no less than explore the inner landscape of the true self.

The Beloved

Your true self is the person whom God thought up and loved from the foundations of the world. It is Christ dwelling within you, literally Christ-in-you, the union of the Spirit of Christ and the human soul. Your true self is the residence of God's love within your very being, re-creating it, sustaining it, making all things new.

And this love is not simply a hallmark or an element of your true self; it is the marrow of who you really are. Brennan Manning points out that the apostle John always identifies himself as "the disciple Jesus loved": "If John were to be asked, 'What is your primary identity, your most coherent sense of yourself?' he would not reply, 'I am a disciple, an apostle, an evangelist,' but 'I am the one Jesus loves.'"[3] When, like John, you have experienced Jesus' love through real and intimate connection, you become anchored more and more in complete identification with the love of God.

And how deep does such identification go? What follows may be the most important sentence in this book: The love of God is who you are, the compassion of Christ is the only solid identity you will ever apprehend. All thoughts of identity apart from this single, magnificent truth are shadow and illusion. The love that God unwaveringly holds for you, received within your immortal soul, is your real identity, your true self. The love of God is everything, and you are nothing apart from this one love. Immersed in your compassionate God, you live and move and have your being (Acts 17:28). Because the love of God is who you are, the most accurate way to think about your true self, the one phrase that can resonate deep within your being, is "I am the beloved of Christ." Can you open yourself to this wondrous truth? You are the beloved. The glory of God is at home in you.

In his book *Life of the Beloved,* Henri Nouwen boils down the spiritual life to that one concept: becoming the beloved. We must all stop racing around trying to build self-definition founded in clay and rust. The love God gratuitously gives is your identity: "You are the beloved." And you must dare to believe this is who you are. You must contradict the numerous voices that would align your personhood with wounds and performance. Your response to God's love is so crucial because the spiritual life begins with identity, and the ultimate significance of your life—all action, each thought, every prayer—is formed and informed by the foundation of identity.

As Nouwen points out, our belovedness is fact—this is our identity—but we also must become the beloved. The journey of the true self is about becoming God's beloved. Nouwen explains what *becoming* means:

> Becoming the Beloved means letting the truth of our Belovedness become enfleshed in everything we think, say or do. It entails a long and painful process of appropriation or, better, incarnation. As long as "being the beloved" is little more than a beautiful thought or a lofty idea that hangs above my life to keep me from becoming depressed, nothing really changes. What is required is to become the Beloved in the commonplaces of my daily existence and, bit by bit, to close the gap that exists between what I know myself to be and the countless specific realities of everyday life. Becoming the Beloved is pulling the truth revealed to me from above down into the ordinariness of what I am, in fact, thinking of, talking about and doing from hour to hour.[4]

Our belovedness, then, cannot remain a magnificent idea that we pull out and mull over on rainy days—it must be a sacred encounter in our daily lives. To the extent that your head and heart both receive your belovedness, you find your true self and begin a life of fiery transformation. The barriers to such a life are many—perhaps you're thinking of them now—and Christian culture provides few signposts for the journey. Living as the beloved may swim against the tide of this culture, but there will be no greater joy than in living your days as Christ's beloved.

Christ and the Unseparate Self

Our true self is Christ-in-me, a beautiful expression of our unity with God through faith. In human encounters, we live with a separation—physically, emotionally, and spiritually—from those we love. In the kingdom of God, however, the beloved cannot be considered apart from the Lover, and this nonseparateness is commonly referred to as being "in Christ."

This state of being "in Christ" is spoken of throughout the New Testament: "It is because of him that you are in Christ Jesus" (1 Cor. 1:30); "There is no condemnation for those who are in Christ Jesus" (Rom. 8:1); and "The glorious riches of this mystery, which is Christ in you, the hope of glory" (Col. 1:27). We were formerly "separate from Christ" but now find our selves "in Christ Jesus" (Eph. 2:12–13).

We are quick to accept the theology of this union of being in Christ, yet our understanding, especially in actual living, of our *in-ness* is often inadequate. We fail to understand the power of the little preposition *in*. As good evangelicals, we're typically on guard against heretical ideas that subtly declare that we ourselves are god. But in our well-founded vigilance, we commit a reactionary heresy, the heresy of separateness from God.

William Shannon draws the line well: "I am distinct from God, for obviously I am not God. But I am not separate, for apart from God I am nothing. . . . This means that I cannot conceive of myself as apart from God. Apart from God, I simply do not exist. I am not there."[5] Christ-in-me, the true self, as spoken of in Scripture, only finds existence in intimate union. Many Christians, however, fear the depth and intensity of *in-ness*. They see union with Christ like oil and vinegar—they share the same jar but separate into distinct entities. Such a perception dismantles the message of Scripture and prevents us from a full understanding of our true-self belovedness. The true self is the self that exists only because God exists, and its existence is completely contingent upon God's. In other words, "I minus God equals zero."[6]

A folktale illustrates the true self's unity with God. One day a young man made his way through the forest to the house of his beloved. Breathless upon arriving and filled with anticipation, he knocked upon the door.

"Who is it?" asked his beloved within.

"It is I!" he cried out.

Came the reply: "There is not enough room in here for me and thee."

The man returned to the forest, discouraged. After thinking on his lover's response, he once again returned to the little house and rapped upon the door.

"Who is it?" inquired the beloved.

"It is thee!" he declared.

His beloved then opened the door and allowed the man to enter.[7]

This little story well demonstrates the unity that exists between Christ and the beloved, your true self. And the unity of the true self and Christ is fact at the moment of salvation. But for most, the way we live our days doesn't declare this unity. We lumber through our activities steeped in individualism and isolation. So often, our prayers are for "God to be with me" in this situation or for "God to be present" in that dilemma. We must stop praying heresies. God couldn't be more with us than he is in this moment. We mistake our inattention for his absence. The lie of our separateness from God prevents many from accepting their belovedness as a working reality.

Leanne Payne suggests that when you sense separateness from Christ to put your hand over your heart and recite a stunning truth: "Another lives in me." Not in theory, not in head knowledge but genuinely, actually, breathing within you right now:

Another lives in me. Our lives are truly transformed only by fully embracing the unity that already exists, by walking re-created in the God-breathed self that is incarnated within us. But most of the time, we fail to function from this blessed reality, blocking the power and presence of this daily grace.

As in the folktale above, you must stand at the house of Jesus the Beloved and cry out, "It is thee!" And as you move in awareness of this unity, you become, mysteriously, actually, Christ to others. Meditate on this portion of St. Patrick's breastplate, an ancient prayer and hymn:

> Christ with me, Christ before me, Christ behind me,
>   Christ in me,
> Christ beneath me, Christ above me, Christ on my right,
>   Christ on my left,
> Christ in breadth, Christ in length, Christ in height,
> Christ in the heart of every man who thinks of me,
> Christ in the mouth of every man who speaks of me,
> Christ in every eye that sees me, Christ in every ear that
>   hears me.

Too, the wondrous words of Paul echo in our hearts: "For I am convinced that neither death nor life, neither angels nor demons, neither the present nor the future, nor any powers, neither height nor depth, nor anything else in all creation, will be able to separate us from the love of God that is in Christ Jesus our Lord" (Rom. 8:38–39). *The love of God that is in Christ Jesus our Lord*—there is nothing else. This love is our hope, our life, our deep and essential self.

In John's gospel, Jesus prays for all believers and foretells their ministry: "I have given them the glory that you gave me, that they may be one as we are one: I in them and you in me. May they be brought to complete unity to let the world know that you sent me and have loved them even as you have loved me" (17:22–23). Jesus desires union, "I in them," an *in-ness* with him that *exactly* mirrors his unity with the Father! It is from this true-self intimacy and union that God intended the world to hear, understand, and respond to the authentic love demonstrated through Jesus. We, the beloved of Christ resting in our ever-constant union with Jesus—are the glory of God who speak healing, wholeness, and life itself to a broken world.

Mapping Out the True Self

By her own account, Julia was raised as a solid, typical evangelical. Her family—involved in an active church—dedicated themselves to duty and to disciplines. She says, "My early adulthood was filled with Scripture memory and Bible study but held little devotion in the full sense of connection and adoration. I had an internal checklist for my devotions that I made up. It was a bondage to self." Since "doing for God" was an expectation, she signed on for a variety of ministries. Once, while in lay leader training with a major parachurch organization, she was invited to write out her testimony from God's perspective, which was a novel idea for her, and something began to shift: "I heard God's heart toward me—loving me, longing for me—a love not just for all people but for me, Julia." An intimacy slowly opened, and she began her journey into the true self.

While certainly not immune to struggle, Julia radiates joy and peace. She's still a tireless minister—her compassionate gift of prayer has mediated the grace of God to hundreds of people. In pondering her journey from false self into true, she remarks, "My quiet time used to be lonely—it was just me doing stuff. There was a strange sense of walking alongside myself noticing how good I was doing and wasn't I special for doing that." As she laughs at such thoughts now, her voice softens. "Now, it's just being with him. In my quiet time lately I've been telling God why I love him—thanking him for continuing to speak to me, for breathing life into me, for causing me to become. I want to love him back intentionally, to make my devotional time a time of intimacy. Recently, I heard his voice say, 'I'm not going to be unequally yoked. You will be a fit partner for me.' That's been undoing me—to be made glorious, to be made a perfect Eve for the second Adam. I'm a bride without spot or blemish. I'm blown away by that. He is the true source of beauty and of being."

Our beloved union with Christ is our shining and awesome true self. And to live our days steeped in that glorious self is our privilege and our destiny as objects of God's affection. This sort of talk is not new—many Christian circles are saturated with it. Yet the number of us who actually function as the beloved for any significant portion of our days is miniscule at best. But the life of the true self is not hidden or difficult. The core of this self's existence can be easily summed up: the life of the true self is bound up in receiving and giving the love of God. The true self is depicted in the following:

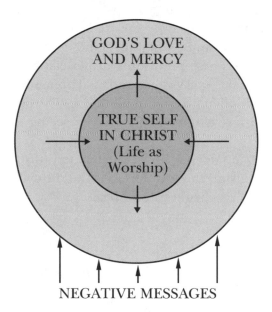

The true self exists within the bosom of God's unfailing love and mercy, where it abides, surrounded and safe. Immersed in God, the true self has found its life. The negative messages remain both as historical fact and as a potential hindrance in the present, but they are banished outside the place of identity and not allowed admittance to the core self. When these negative messages are put in their proper place, God's love may define the self. The arrows pointing in and out of the true self represent the giving and receiving of God's love and mercy vital to the true self's God-centered definition. Anytime we receive or give the authentic love of God, the true self is in residence.

Since the true self has no reality apart from God's love and mercy, the true self emerges when this one supreme love is received. When the true self is called out by love, it responds with love, and the culmination of giving love back to God is a life of worship. And loving God through worship does not refer simply to ascribing worth to God in the smaller corners of our lives, such as weekly church or devotions. That definition of worship is too limiting. The true self's worship is to live in God's presence, meaning to acknowledge and experience him and love him in all of life.

Driving to work can be worship, standing in line at the grocery store can be worship, washing dishes can be worship. For the true self, God is everywhere and, as Thomas Merton notes, his love is the hidden ground of all that is. The life of the true self is a life of love and worship, a life of seeing the divine all around us.

By now delving deeper into the lifeblood of the true self—receiving and giving the love of God—the distortions we hold of God and self can begin to find healing.

Love Received

> You are precious and honored in my sight, and . . . I love you. (Isaiah 43:4)

> As the Father has loved me, so have I loved you. (John 15:9)

> How great is the love the Father has lavished on us, that we should be called children of God! And that is what we are! (1 John 3:1)

Both Scripture and our lives with God make clear that love is the banquet at which we are to daily feast. We are called to taste and to touch the embrace of God. Through venturing into the true self, we come to understand that love is truly the only currency that matters and that receiving God's love is our primary spiritual responsibility. Only when God's love has been genuinely received can the true self be called out and enabled to give away this love in worshipful living.

Within Christian culture, our approach to contemporary discipleship encourages a *type* of true-self living: loving God and neighbor. I have sat through sermons, conferences, and Sunday school classes exhorting me to put love into action, reminding me that love is the one ultimate mark of the believer, urging me into service to my neighbor. Almost everyone, it seems, starts the movement of love at square B—giving love. I've rarely heard anyone begin at square A—receiving love—which is ground zero, the necessary foundation from which all else follows.

Any exhortation to love God and others that is divorced from a call to first receive the love of God is not just incomplete, it has little objective reality. Still, this type of discipleship is almost universally advocated. We are rarely, if ever, taught how to receive the love that calls out the true self. Herein lies the problem for many of us who would follow Christ: We have no idea how to experience the love of God, how to take it in, how to rest in the compassion that called us into being. It's no wonder there's so much talk about love and so little loving: There's precious little true-self living.

Part of our problem in receiving God's love is that we recognize, and rightly so, that we aren't that lovable. As a frail, inconsistent creature, how can the love of a perfect and holy God be freely mine? My false self says, "It's not"—which is why I must perform or hide. But as a maturing believer I must accept that God loves differently than I do. Brennan Manning explains that as humans we love because we discover something pleasing within people and things and respond to it with our favor or appreciation. But that's not the way God loves: "Unlike ourselves, the Father of Jesus loves men and women, not for what He finds in them, but for what lies within Himself. . . . He does not detect what is congenial, appealing, attractive, and respond to it with His favor. In fact, He does not respond at all. The Father of Jesus is a source. He acts; He does not react. He initiates love. He is love without motive."[8]

God loves you because he is love. To participate in God is to partake of love. Rightly understood, receiving the love of God is not an extravagance or a frill meant to hover on the periphery of your devotional life. Manning states the incredible: "The most important thing that ever happens in prayer is letting ourselves be loved by God."[9] God's love received is the core, the place from which all else finds purpose and fullness.

But for many of us, discussions about receiving and giving God's love bring tension, sadness, even pain. Perhaps the negative messages—wounds inflicted by circumstance or by others— have left us jaded and frustrated, fearful of opening again to God's love. The risk of love, however, must be taken because, honestly, we've no place else to go and because apart from God's love we're all shadowy players, haphazardly walking through our roles on the stage of life. The love of God alone is meaning and substance.

As I journey with God into my middle years, I realize that all that I am and all that I do must begin with the reception of God's love. When I do not treat this receiving as the serious spiritual discipline that it is, I notice a hollowness in what I give to others, even if I am actually "accomplishing" more. Henri Nouwen notes, "The greatest gift I have to offer is my own joy of living, my own inner peace, my own silence and solitude, my own sense of well-being."[10] Nouwen's words sound like another language in a culture—and I mean a Christian culture—where tangible productivity is the main marker of spiritual stature and maturity. Through letting ourselves be loved by God and through loving him back, we possess Presence in our presence. There is no greater offering we can bring to life or ministry, and the world is dying for lack of it.

Loving God

Once the love of God has been deeply and thoroughly received, the possibility of loving God back exists in each moment. Of course, such loving reaches into our doing—the ways in which worship is expressed in all facets of life—but it must begin in our being. Our true self loves God simply for his magnificent being, and for our true self, there is nothing more natural, more congruent, than to spend each day loving our Creator.

Have you ever wondered how God sees this return of love? Our freely loving God in the self whom he created has great value to him. Just as a child's affectionate scrawls in crayon are of inestimable value to the parent, even our feeblest expressions of genuine love are treasured and have sway over God's heart. Having received God's love, we have something very personal and entirely unique to give back to God, something he cherishes—our response of love. James Finley beautifully describes the heavenly reaction to our authentic love for God:

> The first and most important commandment is to "love God with all your heart, with all your soul, and all your mind" (Matt. 22:37). The contemplative work of the Spirit is the carrying out of this commandment whereby you give God the greatest delight. His joy is in knowing this: My child is loving me. My child has discovered why I created persons—that they might be one with me in loving me as I love them. In this moment of turning to God in detached love all the angels and saints stop, turn to you and listen: Someone is loving God for his own sake. Someone has discovered the love that is eternal life. There is a kind of heavenly rush hour as all the citizens of heaven come to aid you in loving God. . . . The devils rage over this simple love, for it touches the raw edge of their anguish, which is their refusal and subsequent helplessness to love God.[11]

Have you experienced the sweetness of receiving the love of God and his delight in you as you love him? It's what you were made for, your heart's home. Like the deer panting for cool streams, your true self's very existence lies in drinking deeply of the living water of God's love.

How often have we prayed the Lord's Prayer and breezed over the phrase, "Your will be done on earth as it is in heaven"? What is the will of God? We tend to think of the will of God in terms of decisions: taking this job, marrying this person, moving to such and such a location, involving ourselves in one ministry or another, one church or another. While God's will certainly extends to these concerns, such things form the barest crust of God's will. Listen to Jeanne Guyon speak on that little phrase from the Lord's prayer: "His will is that His children love Him. Therefore, when you pray, 'Lord, Your will be done,' you are actually asking the Lord to allow you to *love* Him. So begin to love Him! And as you do, beseech Him to give you His love."[12] God's will at its most basic and profound is that we receive and give his love. All else flows, and only contains meaning, in light of this tender and holy exchange.

What does this giving and receiving look like? How do we *do* it? It is not something we accomplish but something we are. Radical in its simplicity, we merely come present to the love of God that is our being.

One June morning, I went about my typical devotional time with God. My usual practice is to worship a little, listen to the Scriptures, and have a time of intercession and quiet prayer. This particular day I programmed two worship songs on my stereo to help me open my awareness to the presence of God and to receive. What happened is unexplainable. I wasn't feeling especially spiritual, but by the second song, "I Could Sing of Your Love Forever," I was absorbed in God's loving presence. The song kept repeating, "I could sing of your love forever" over and over, and the words were in me—in a sense, the words were me. The song slowly faded, and I just sat there. In stillness. Completely immersed in the Lord. I can't explain it any clearer than this: My true self, in a very tangible way, was held in the arms of Jesus, and the experience was me, and I was keenly present to it all.

I'm not sure how long I sat there, but my false self eventually sent a telegram: "The worship portion of your quiet time has been completed and shouldn't you move on in your little devotional program?" I was tempted—but only for a second. No, I waved the interruption away like a gnat. The reason I even had a devotional time—conscious union with my Beloved—was wonderfully mine then and there with no effort on my part. I simply sat in the presence of God, loving him, receiving his love. It was incredibly sweet and intimate. There was nowhere to go, nothing more to do. Like Mary curled up at the feet of Jesus, I had found the one thing necessary.

And later, I thought about how countercultural it is to just receive love and love God back, to just be, and have that being be my identity. Sadly, our usual circles of faith, tainted by the false self, would rarely be still long enough to taste what I had just experienced.

And I thought about something Thomas Merton said. A few times in my life, I've read something and instantly known that my life lived on the other side of those words would never be the same. Merton is talking about prayer, but his thoughts can be expanded to the whole spiritual journey into the true self:

> We were indoctrinated so much into means and ends that we don't realize that there is a different dimension in the life of prayer. In technology you have this horizontal progress, where you must start at one point and move to another and then another. But that is not the way to build a life of prayer. In prayer we discover what we already have. And you realize that you are already there. We already have everything, but we don't know it and we don't experience it. Everything has been given to us in Christ. All we need is to experience what we already possess. The trouble is we aren't taking time to do so.[13]

You will never have more of Jesus than you do at this moment. If you are in Christ, you are already at your final destination. There's no place else to go, no progress from point A to point B, because there is no point B. There is only point A, and more of A, which is to say, there is only Jesus and more of Jesus until his love envelops all that you are, defines all that you are, and is powerfully expressed in everything you touch. If the thought that you've already reached your destination disappoints you in any way, don't despair. Pray that you will become fully opened to what already is. In this present moment, the glorious life and love of Christ already resides within you by faith. It is the sum total of all you've ever wanted in your heart of hearts.

Images of God and Self: Finding Wholeness

When you discover this place of love and your life begins to revolve more and more around receiving and giving God's love, your sense of self begins to heal. People whose true self is emerging have experienced all the same negative messages that create the false self, but the true-self-emerging person is participating in ongoing healing from these lies. Christian culture tends to promote a self-help approach to such transformation—read this book, attend this conference, take more notes during the sermon. Such things are helpful, but Merton asserts that we simply need to experience what we already possess; at core, the healing that we most desperately need comes only from dwelling in the love of God.

And while we can put ourselves in a place to receive this healing, we cannot initiate or control it. The healing of our self-image comes about as we enter God's most intimate will for our lives—receiving and giving the love of God. In such an encounter our souls become whole because healing is not so much something God does, it is who God is. When you open your awareness to God, when you walk in his presence, healing is as near as your next heartbeat.

And what is the evidence of this healing in your life? Self-acceptance. For some of us, this is a frightening word, because we associate self-acceptance with license to sin or permission to wallow in our character defects. Self-hatred is the fence that keeps our lives within orderly boundaries. Self-acceptance, we fear, stunts growth in holiness. This view comes directly from the typewriter of the false self. As the last chapter pointed out, self-hatred, which is the opposite of self-acceptance, fuels our self-absorbed narcissism. The false self fears talk of self-acceptance because it knows that without self-hatred dominating the consciousness, the false self will cease to exist.

Self-acceptance, says Leanne Payne, is an "authentic and necessary Christian virtue."[14] Self-acceptance gives assent to be who I am—a small, limited person with bents toward sin as well as hungers for holiness—and allows me to live with all my contradictions, because my will, at least on my good days, is to "walk in the light, as he is in the light" (1 John 1:7). To walk in the light, then, is to live our life, our *whole* life, under the eye of God, in communion with him. When our lives unfold in such a place—which is the kingdom of God—we can appropriate God's gentleness, kindness, and loving acceptance of all that we are. He makes it possible for us to embrace these qualities in our attitudes toward ourselves. Godly self-acceptance, then, emerges simply from dwelling in God's presence, rather than in accomplishing a list of self-accepting behaviors.

But the crux of the healing of self-image and the emerging of our true selves is the receiving and giving of God's love. Perhaps at first this journey is a tentative one as our old views of God and self still haunt our acquaintanceship with our true selves. Perhaps it's even like Kirkegaard's leap of faith over forty thousand fathoms of dark water. But from such a leap comes the healing of our souls, and within this intimate friendship with God, we also mysteriously find healing for our image of God.

When Jesus finished the Sermon on the Mount, he descended and met a leper. The story is told in Matthew 8: "When he came down from the mountainside, large crowds followed him.

A man with leprosy came and knelt before him and said, 'Lord, if you are willing, you can make me clean.' Jesus reached out his hand and touched the man. 'I am willing,' he said. 'Be clean!' Immediately he was cured of his leprosy" (vv. 1–3).

"If you are willing, you can make me clean." The leper was convinced that Jesus could free him of his disease. But within his statement is embedded a pivotal question. Would the Lord be willing to help one such as him, a man covered with odious sores, a man who broke Jewish law just by entering the perimeter of the community? How far does the compassion of God go? The leper was saying, "Yes, God is all-powerful, but is he truly good?"

This is the foundational question each of us must ask: Do I believe God is good? We all know the "right" response is to say, "Yes, of course, the Bible clearly tells me God is good." But what about the God we relate to, not intellectually but actually? Do you ever fear hearing from God in prayer because you're afraid of what he might say to you? Do you move through your life sensing that God is disappointed in you or unhappy with you? Or do you quietly steel yourself toward God because you sense at some point he's going to lower the boom on you for all your wrongs? If you answer "yes" to any of these questions, then you do not believe God is entirely good. You have a distorted view of God.

Like the leper, the messages of our personal woundedness relegate us to the borderline of mercy from a god who possesses a limited or capricious regard for us. Desiring to live in the true self does not automatically heal our image of God. It's a slow conversion, where we must confront the cardboard cutouts of God to which we have bowed down.

But we're not strong enough to set aside these false images, not powerful enough to heal our images of God or of ourselves. We can't do enough right behaviors or spiritual gymnastics to convince ourselves of God's goodness. Our healing comes from encountering God's love for us, an encounter that he initiates. All we can do is put ourselves in a place to receive what God has for us. And what will we find when we do? Infinite tenderness, compassion, and the realization that God is so very glad to live within our hearts, so very pleased that we possess even the smallest flicker of faith. Meditate upon the following questions, because within them is revealed the heart of God toward you in this moment:

> Do you ever reflect upon the fact that Jesus feels proud of you? Proud that you accepted the faith which he offered you? Proud that you chose him for a friend and Lord? Is proud of you that you haven't given up? Proud that you believe in him enough to try again and again? Proud that you trust he can help you? Do you ever think that Jesus appreciates you for wanting him, for wanting to say no to so many things that would separate you from him? Do you think that Jesus can ever be grateful to you for pausing to smile, comfort, give to one of his children who have such great need to see a smile, to feel a touch? Do you think that Jesus can ever be grateful to you for learning more about him so that you can speak to others more deeply and truly about him?[15]

The idea that God feels tenderness toward us, desires intimate friendship, is proud of us and appreciates us, is unfathomable for many. But, like the leper, we must approach this Christ we barely recognize, hampered as we are with doubts and fear, to experience who this God really is.

In such a moment, the schism between the head and the heart reaches its ultimate showdown: We know God loves us but we don't experience that love, and our heart only believes what it experiences. The true self needs both head and heart to be opened to, and convinced of, God's love and goodness. And as the head and heart inch toward the same magnificent conclusion, we realize the love of God is all around us, holding together all that is, closer to us than we are to ourselves. Our distortions of God and self meet the risen Christ and are gradually clarified by holy encounter.

Jesus is as present and attentive to you in this moment as he was to the cleansed leper who never again needed to wonder if God was good. The leper's whole identity changed with one touch from the Savior, and his story is a powerful metaphor of what happens when you and I, too, come to Jesus in all our wretchedness and insufficiency. You no longer need to be defined by rags and woundedness and falsity. Through his touch of love, his willing heart, you may become your true identity—a beloved person who is healed, whole, and holy.

Saying Yes to Belovedness

I was once asked to participate in a panel discussion, and I happened to share my spiritual identity as the beloved, and how I took seriously, literally, my spousal relationship with God. Afterward, I talked with a woman with whom I was acquainted and whose spiritual life I respected. She made reference to my remarks about being the beloved and said, "You know, I tried the whole God-as-my-husband thing, and it didn't work for me." She defined belovedness solely in terms of romantic human relationships. Besides, she added, we have Jesus as Guide and Master and isn't that enough? I replied with something profound like "Oh," because I was too stunned to respond. Her comment was as casual as if she'd said, "You know, I once tried sushi but didn't care for it." Outwardly, the conversation closed, but discord reigned inside me.

Later, I found myself wanting to revisit that conversation, and shout, not out of anger but urgency, "Being the beloved is the most ultimate, the most real, the most powerful and precious identity you will ever walk in! Apart from this identity, you have nothing, you are nothing, and you say it didn't 'work' for you? How can that be?" That encounter pulled back an outer layer of spirituality for me, revealing a sad and startling truth: Many sincere, Bible-toting Christians have no desire to be the beloved in anything except in some airy idea-land.

From Israel's rejection of God when they demanded a human king in 1 Samuel; to the religious elite who searched diligently for God in the Scriptures while refusing to come to Jesus; to my friend's declaration that, in the real world, God as our beloved spouse isn't necessary—the people of God through the ages have repeatedly said "no" to God's invitation for intimate communion. Affirming our belovedness means receiving into our meager frames the fiery passion of God. Perhaps we intrinsically understand that becoming God's beloved will demand everything, will alter everything, and we shrink back from such overwhelming and all-consuming affection.

Every moment, the vulnerability of God displays itself in Jesus' question to Peter by the seashore: "Do you love me?" In the history of religions, no other god opens himself to human rejection in all its insidious forms: from our insistence for a real king—or to be king ourselves—to our desire for the love of God to be manifest in human form only. Henri Nouwen says,

> The unfathomable mystery of God is that God is a Lover who wants to be loved. The one who created us is waiting for our response to the love that gave us our being. God not only says: "You are my Beloved." God also asks: "Do you love me?" and offers us countless chances to say "Yes" to our inner truth. The spiritual life, thus understood, radically changes everything. Being born and growing up, leaving home and finding a career, being praised and being rejected, walking and resting, praying and playing, becoming ill and being healed—yes, living and dying—they all become expressions of that divine question: "Do you love me?" And at every point of the journey there is the choice to say "yes" and the choice to say "no."[16]

This belovedness is not an ethereal idea reserved for Sundays. It is our real self, a living, burning reality that will fulfill our deepest desires. The call to God's openhearted longing to be our Beloved, to love him, to receive him, in the same vulnerable, intimate way a wife does a husband, beckons us now in this moment.

Here, spiritual formation is stripped down to its most basic and vital question, a query we must answer daily: Do you truly believe Jesus is enough? That is, is the love of God sufficient to satisfy the hungers of your heart? Is Christ really all you want and need? Is God alone lover enough to eternally forsake all rivals?

The Lord says, "I will betroth you to me forever; I will betroth you in righteousness and justice, in love and compassion. I will betroth you in faithfulness, and you will acknowledge the LORD" (Hos. 2:19–20). Nouwen might well have been speaking of the journey into the true self when he wrote, "The change of which I speak is the change from living life as a painful test to prove that you deserve to be loved, to living it as an unceasing 'Yes' to the truth of that Belovedness."[17] And in living that belovedness, not just theoretically but actually, are wondrous delights, unspeakable gladness, and restful love.

In light of all that is temporal and fractured in this world, it only makes sense to allow the compassion of Christ alone to form our identities. But how do we say "yes" to being the beloved, to entering that holy of holies, to receiving the gift of our true selves? Anyone claiming to offer prescriptions for how to fall in love should be treated with great suspicion. And that's what the true self is all about—falling deeply, madly in love with God. For entering such holiness there is no formula, no grand scheme.

C. S. Lewis gives us great wisdom: "Your real, new self (which is Christ's and also yours, and yours just because it is His) will not come as long you are looking for it. It will come when you are looking for Him."[18] Thus, as true-self-emerging persons, we must seek God for his own sake, not for a new self or a healed self or anything else we might want from him. But in as much as we are being healed and made new by the seeking, we are able more and more to live in the presence of God. You cannot create the journey, you can only accept Christ's invitation, allowing him to be the axis around which all else revolves. Here, we move from "It is I" to "It is Thee," a life of divine desire.

Andre Seve says, "Either hunger for God is the sun around which I organize everything; or else God is just one object among others orbiting the very crowded sky of my life." Which is true for you? Which do you want to be true? For those who would choose Christ as the center, the remainder of this book will suggest what a God-hungry life, a true-self life, might look like.

To live and move in the true self is as close to heaven as we can come here on earth, and of such people is the kingdom of God comprised, both above and below. By God's good grace, let us continue the pilgrimage. Love, acceptance, communion, joy—all these are daily offered to us as pure gifts as we rest in our real identities before the Lord. We need not chase after what we most desire—it's already ours. We need not wonder where the overwhelming love of God hides—his love *is* our true self. The journey home is not a long one. When you and I come present to Christ-in-me, we're already there.

6

BLESSING AND KINGDOM LIVING

The Way of Brokenness

The sacrifices of God are a broken spirit;
a broken and contrite heart,
O God, you will not despise.

—*Psalm 51:17*

We must learn the art of weakness, of non-achievement,
of being able to cope with the knowledge of our own poverty and
helplessness, without trying to escape from it into something we
can accept more easily.

—*Simon Tugwell*

A bruised reed he will not break,
and a smoldering wick he will not snuff out.

—*Isaiah 42:3*

You need only claim the events of your life to make yourself
yours. When you truly possess all you have been and done . . .
you are fierce with reality.

—*Florida Scott-Maxwell*

It was a Friday night, and I was on a church retreat at a camp in Minnesota. The speaker outlined our task—make a collage of our lives to share later in small groups. A mountain of old magazines was on hand from which to snip bits and pieces to cover our white poster board.

I set about cutting out words and pictures that had meaning in my journey, words such as *life* and *God,* glossy pictures of children, nature, cars, and other things. In the midst of perusing the magazines, I found a photo of a religious painting. It depicted a crippled beggar, lying on a mat, crutch by his side. He was reaching up toward Jesus, who stood over him and was reaching his hand down to meet the beggar's. Something in the picture touched me. I liked it, felt as though it belonged, and pasted it on my collage.

Later, I gathered with a few other participants to share our collages. By now it was getting late, and I was tired after a hectic day of work and travel. My turn came, and I briefly explained the various items glued to my poster board. When I got to the painting of Jesus and the beggar, I pointed at it and, without thinking, said, "This is me on my best day."

My own words startled me. Through those simple words about a magazine photo, I had stumbled into something profound, and those words have been engraved on my life ever since. My realization was this: on my best day, in my biggest and brightest hour, at my most competent moment possible, I am the crippled beggar for whom Jesus stopped. No matter how many talents I think I have, no matter how powerful I may believe myself to be, in reality, I am the one lying on a mat, sorely in need of the loving touch of Jesus of Nazareth.

Within the kingdom of God, I have come to understand that the way of the true self is the way of poverty, that insufficiency is reason to rejoice, that wounds and limitations are the path to empowerment, that ministry flows from the childlike who revel in their smallness, who know if Jesus doesn't stop for them, there's no hope, no life, nothing. This is not a curse that limits but a truth that liberates. It's good news. The true self is the beloved, but it is also broken. Brokenness is blessing.

And most of us don't believe a word of it.

Poverty in the Kingdom

One thing about us can be said for certain: We are weak and wounded people. I am impoverished. You are impoverished. Our weakness is simply our human condition as fragile, incomplete creatures. My weaknesses emerge frequently—overblown reactions to trivial offenses, petty thoughts and judgments, fatigue, emotional limits. Out of this human vulnerability, wounds—physical, emotional, spiritual—scar my history. I have a laundry list—friendships that shut down, rejections from those I wanted to love me, deaths of important people, remarks that slapped me at key moments, physical constraints from age and injury.

You can probably identify. Wounds and weakness are the common denominators, the poverty that mark our lives on earth. Human weakness is not specifically our sin nature, although in our weakness, we certainly do sin. And wounds are often the result of sin—either ours or someone else's. We've been devastated through our human vulnerability and left with hearts shredded by our fallen world. The truth is, if we're honest, we all know what it's like to be the crippled beggar on the mat. We just prefer not to acknowledge it.

But our wounds and weaknesses are entirely ours. Denying them doesn't change their being firmly woven into the fabric of our being. They speak of things that are deeply true and very personal, creating significant markers within our stories. Sometimes, it feels as if they *are* our stories. Our wounds and weakness are spliced throughout our history, so the posture we choose toward our poverty matters.

Americans, Christian or not, wrestle with the poverty that makes us human, vacillating between ignoring it and despising it. We are a nation of highly individualistic people who idolize the self-made man or woman. We are largely the children of immigrants who pulled themselves up by their bootstraps, spiritually and otherwise, and many among us have inherited a legacy in which things emotional were discounted. Self-reflection and self-care were often labeled as selfish, and rest, even spiritual rest, was considered old-fashioned laziness. In the middle of this ethos, a high value was placed upon independence and self-sufficiency, both of which ignore most of our genuine neediness, especially the needs of our souls.

Our culture today pushes us toward an obsession with self-mastery and self-competence. Gerald May speaks of our peculiar difficulties with accepting limitations of any kind:

> In some other culture, in a society that reveres the mystery of human nature more than ours does, such failures at self-mastery might not be so devastating. They might even be seen as affirmation of one's essential connectedness with the rest of creation and one's essential dependency upon the Creator. But in modern Western society, we have come to see ourselves as objects of our own creation. When we fail at managing ourselves, we feel defective.[1]

In our culture, it is not safe to be weak. Our weakness does not serve to bind us to God and to others; it divides, keeping us in denial and in hiding. And we are terrified that people will see our poverty, that others will label us as incompetent, that someone will learn our dreaded secret: We don't measure up; we are impoverished. We fear facing our wounds and living with limitations because culture tells us that broken is, well, just broken. There's no remedy for it, and that which is weak gets trampled by the powerful.

But in regard to poverty and the life of faith, what should our response be? By and large, the church tends to see poverty as contrary to the life of wholeness and abundance to which Christ calls us. But is that what the Scriptures teach? The philosophy that wounds and weakness are always at odds with our life in Christ emerges from false-self culture and not Scripture. After God told the apostle Paul that "my grace is sufficient for you, for my power is made perfect in weakness," Paul responds, "Therefore I will boast all the more gladly about my weaknesses, so that Christ's power may rest on me. . . . For when I am weak, then I am strong" (2 Cor. 12:9–10).

We hear these verses and likely patronize them with a nod of the head without ever marveling at how contrary they are to our typical behavior. Paul has experienced something extraordinary here: bragging about his weakness because Jesus' power is manifested in such places. In light of how we think about weakness—and how weak we really are—we have to ask how it is possible that Paul responded in this way. Paul recognized and rejoiced in something terribly curious—a spiritual connection between weakness and the power of Christ to flow through us.

Jesus' teaching on poverty and the kingdom goes even further. The Sermon on the Mount, Christ's great manifesto on life in the kingdom of God, was delivered at the brink of Jesus' entry into the public eye. While still early in his ministry life, news about him had spread everywhere. Jesus was the latest wave in Palestine. He preached and healed many, and great crowds jostled around him while the false-self power brokers within the disciples rubbed their hands together in great delight. In the midst of the growing, circus-type atmosphere, they must have been surprised, stunned even, to hear the first teaching out of Jesus' mouth on that hillside: "Blessed are the poor in spirit, for theirs is the kingdom of heaven" (Matt. 5:3).

The Greek word for "poor in spirit" is *ptochos,* which means "with reference to the spirit, a poverty." Going further into its extended nuances, *ptochos* indicates "one who is reduced to a begging dependence, one who is broken." The typical word for *poor* in Jesus' day was *penacross,* but Jesus chose the word *ptochos,* which is a much more extreme and intense form of the word *poor. Penacross* might describe a man who, while very poor, manages to fend for himself, digging through garbage cans to find enough to eat. He's poor but he gets by. As *ptochos,* the man is so poor, so weak, so destitute, that he lies in the gutter, and if someone doesn't stop to help him, he will wither and die.[2] A *ptochos* person is a broken person. And it is broken people, the ones who understand they are poor and helpless, who are given the keys to God's kingdom. Our Western minds can scarcely take it in. But staggering as is such a revelation, Jesus says that there is a first necessary quality of the people who are to inherit his kingdom: brokenness.

Brokenness, then, is a spiritual condition that emerges from our wounds and weakness, a *ptochos,* "poor in spirit," state with our poverty. This brokenness consists of two parts. First, we live in awareness of our wounds and weakness and the sin that so easily ushers from them. We're in the gutter—insufficient and powerless—and we know it. Second, we respond to this poverty by coming to the end of ourselves—our own energy, talents, and intelligence—and realizing, with our total being, that our only hope for life, for change, and for meaning is Jesus Christ.[3] Our posture is one of "begging dependence" upon God. We know we can't accomplish the work of God in and of ourselves. We are impoverished and in dire need of help. We need a Savior. This owning of poverty and clinging to Christ within poverty is brokenness.

Imagine it. The first and foundational kingdom value that Jesus imparted is that the people who own the kingdom, the people to whom its gifts come and through whom its power arises, are not the shining people of faith who appear flawless and without need. No, the kingdom is owned by, and its power comes to those, who know they don't measure up, to those who are willing to embrace weakness, to people who intimately understand their begging dependence upon a merciful Savior.

We are all certainly impoverished. All of us have wounds and weakness. But not all of us are broken. Many Christians choose a cultural response to poverty, instead of a spiritual one. We reject brokenness as a kingdom value, believing it to be negative thinking or part of our victim-centered culture. Some of us fear brokenness because a distorted image of God makes such a state unsafe. Others of us hear about the value of brokenness and, in a superficial response, seek a huge, emotionally charged breaking, or we go around attempting to manufacture brokenness by being sorry for this sin or for that failing. Doing so is a manipulation of true brokenness and a strategy that easily produces a counterfeit brokenness. Brokenness is, at base, surrendering to God our entire being, and we cannot experience it on our own terms.

The idea of brokenness is least foreign when we think of salvation. Much of the teaching we're given is that being poor in spirit is a theological necessity when we pray for salvation, but after that self-mastery takes over. True, in order for authentic regeneration to occur, we must be saturated with the reality of our weaknesses, forays into sin, and wayward desires. But the "poor in spirit" Jesus speaks of sees brokenness as an integral part of all aspects of the spiritual life, because brokenness keeps us dependent upon Christ as the one true Source of life and transformation.

Yet we too often allow the performing false self to steer our faith toward that which keeps it alive—competition.

Competition and the Myth of Competence

Competition surrounds us constantly. It's the basis of capitalism, of our educational system, of running a corporation, and of our sports-crazed culture, whether Little League or the World Series. The media bombards us with one-upmanship—the right shoes or deodorant keeps us a cut above the crowd. We compare everything: clothes, haircuts, bodies, cars, houses, jobs, skills. We nurse jealousies over another's good fortune or move our peg up a notch when we're the conquering hero. We engineer our identity based on competition.

People of faith seem no less affected by competition than the average pagan. Our churches compete in terms of grand architecture and effective programs. Within congregations, we

squirrel away envy or arrogance over who is called to lead, chosen to sing the solo, or recognized for spiritual giftedness.

In the book, *Compassion*, Henri Nouwen, Donald McNeill,
and Douglas Morrison speak of how our primary framework
for life is competition, instead of compassion. When competition is our framework, it organizes reality and constructs our
self-definition. Competition is a natural consequence of living
in the false-self system, which must seek selfhood from that
which surrounds it. Nouwen, Morrison, and McNeill illumine
the ways we gain identity through competition:

> Our whole sense of self is dependent upon the way we
> compare ourselves with others and upon the differences
> we can identify. When the question "Who am I?" is put
> to the powers of this world. . . . The answer is simply,
> "You are the difference you make." It is by our differ-
> ences, distinctions, that we are recognized, honored,
> rejected, or despised. Whether we are more or less in-
> telligent, practical, strong, fast, handy, or handsome
> depends upon those with whom we are compared or
> those with whom we compete. It is upon these positive
> or negative distinctions that much of our self-esteem
> depends. . . . After all, who are we if we cannot proudly
> point to something that sets us apart from others?[4]

Better than, less than—such comparisons are given too much
power to form our self-definition. Indeed, apart from competitive measurements, we might have no idea who we are. False-
self culture demands that we tie a sense of self to external
comparisons. Because church culture has largely acquiesced to
the larger culture, it gives lip service about being a child of
God while never confronting the competitive framework.

When the false-self identity revolves around competition, the
results are spiritually disastrous. Our thought patterns become
an endless series of judgments that emanate, without any real
effort, from a continuous stream of critical observations.

Whether it's a coworker who makes too many personal calls or the family next door torn apart by adultery, we brim with judgments. And why? Our judgments divide reality into success and failure so that our false self finds definition. Like a tick that sucks its lifeblood from a dog, the false self sucks a sense of identity from its environment, and more so, from the ways that reality is judged within the environment. If we are trapped in the performing or degraded false self, then successes and failures must be compulsively calculated.

The competitive system is automatically at odds with the kingdom value of brokenness. In the competitive system, brokenness is failure. What counts is success: to be a winner, to avoid weakness and neediness, to perform well enough to be thought of as whole. But, of course, this system is anchored in the false self, which has no objective reality. In truth, our ideas about success and failure are human-made illusions that have no real meaning in God's kingdom. In the end, we cannot have two frameworks of reality. We cannot in the same moment embrace both the frameworks of kingdom brokenness and that of competition.

When competition is pulled into the life of faith, brokenness is viewed as distinctly unsuccessful and a block to spirituality, rather than seen as a means to Christian growth and maturity. Sometime between Bible skits I observed as a youngster and the theology classes I sat through in college, I came to possess a peculiar idea—that growth and sanctification meant easing into a life where doubts and defects of character were gently erased like a pencil to paper. Christian maturity meant that, year after year, I would outgrow my vulnerabilities, insecurities, and moments of darkness. For most Christians, spiritual maturity is like a ladder that ever ascends to holier air and more heavenly perfection.

Even now, I find myself surprised at the struggles that older Christians endure. Henri Nouwen, in one of his last published reflections, speaks of his struggle:

There was a time when I said, "Next year I will finally have it together," or "When I grow more mature these moments of inner darkness will go," or "Age will diminish my emotional needs." But now I know that my sorrows are mine and will not leave me. . . . The adolescent struggle to find someone to love me is still there; unfulfilled needs for affirmation as a young adult remain alive in me. The deaths of my mother and many family members during my later years cause me continual grief. Beyond all that, I experience deep sorrow that I have not become who I wanted to be, and that the God to whom I have prayed so much has not given me what I have most desired.[5]

These are hard words to hear. When I first encountered this passage from my respected mentor, a shock of disillusionment and desolation shot through my spirit. I felt lost and a little afraid. *Shouldn't he be over such things by now?* I thought. And then I realized that I possessed an erroneous expectation—that really godly people eventually get over their brokenness. I came to understand how competition saturates the life of faith through the myth of competence.

The myth of competence is an unspoken assumption that as I grow and learn in my Christian life, I will become less needy, less dependent, less vulnerable and magically turn into a person who is wise, looks good, and "has her act together." Born of my performing false self, this myth permeated much of my motivation to participate in weekly worship services, attend conferences, spiritual-life workshops, and the like. I might have attended such things to deepen my devotion to Christ, but I also secretly hoped to become a stronger, more capable, and more admired Christian.

But I had things turned around. In actuality, spiritual maturity is a growth toward more dependence, more vulnerability, and a deeper understanding of how paltry my concept of God and his ways really are. This myth of competence generally reigns in faith communities because so many people are caught in the performing false self. But it is the enemy of true Christian growth and holiness.

In my Christian upbringing, I was taught that brokenness only applied to my conversion. After the starting gate, competitive competence took over, and I was subtly instructed to move away from my poverty. Because I was now in the fold and growing spiritually, wounds and weakness became a useless appendage that needed to atrophy and drop off. Discipleship meant Bible studies, seminars, books, personal quiet times. The overt message was that such resources would help me draw near to God and equip me for spiritual battle in a dark world. But the covert message had to do with fashioning me into a shining person of faith, a person perfected by spiritual training so that fewer and fewer chinks marred the armor.

We're all haunted by some image of the perfect Christian—the person who is rarely ruffled, full of right answers, and tirelessly "there" for everyone. Such people glide through life with a two-inch gap between their feet and the ground. They pray for ten hours a day and can recite the entire New Testament over coffee. And, most important, they seem to have no needs, no obvious wounds and weakness. They're always cheerful, never touched by depression, loneliness, or other heavy emotions. Such ones are supposed to be attractive to nonbelievers and spur on weaker Christians with their otherworldliness. And some among us are desperate that others believe this image is who they really are.

But, in the end, the threads of such an image always lead back to the false self. And the false self in one person attracts the false self within others, steeping them in a life of spiritualized unreality. In truth, the phantom Christian does not exist, cannot exist, and any motivation to utilize spiritual resources other than for the pure love of God is bankrupt. The covert messages to strive toward a perfectly executed faith walk emanate from a false-self Christianity wherein needs and brokenness are at odds with what the spiritual life is truly about. If we use spiritual resources to become less needy and less vulnerable, we are caught in the myth of competence. Such a life is not the gospel.

Blessed Brokenness

"Fine," you might say, "maybe brokenness is helpful in the kingdom. But brokenness as blessed? That seems like a stretch." The myth of competence sees brokenness as a condition that points away from true godliness and Christian maturity, in other words, away from a state of blessedness. And to one degree or another, most of us view brokenness this way.

But, in Matthew 5:3, Jesus says, "*Blessed* are the poor in spirit." Jesus called brokenness blessed—and he needed to because we see brokenness as cursed. One of the things Jesus does in the Beatitudes, as well as in the Sermon on the Mount, is to accurately label reality—what's blessed, what's cursed, what's valuable, what's not—because our vision of what's desirable is, at best, skewed. And our brokenness is blessed because Christ himself was willingly broken on our behalf: "He was despised and rejected by men, a man of sorrows, and familiar with suffering. . . . He was pierced for our transgressions, he was crushed for our iniquities; the punishment that brought us peace was upon him" (Isa. 53:3, 5). Jesus' suffering and resurrection and his posture toward his brokenness give us hope for how our own brokenness can be lived as blessing.

While Jesus' earthly ministry was one of life and hope and healing, there was much more to come. Jesus said, "It is for your good that I am going away" (John 16:7) and where he went was to heavenly glory. But the path was through the cross, his ultimate experience of physical and spiritual brokenness. And the power, the ministry, that would flow from Resurrection Sunday altered the world forever. Through his brokenness, his most powerless moment, came healing, restoration, and the great outpouring of love and power from the Father. Jesus' brokenness became our salvation and our eternal blessing.

Do you ever marvel that Jesus' postresurrection body bears the scars of his earthly woundedness? As God, Jesus could have had any body he wanted when he emerged victorious from the tomb. But he kept a wounded body that mirrored his earthly one. And it was by his wounds that he was clearly identified by his disciples as Jesus the Messiah. Even after great triumph, Jesus chose—and, I believe, continues to choose—to remain steadfast in his identity and solidarity with the broken lambs of his flock. We, then, need not be ashamed or desolate in our poverty. He refused to disdain his human woundedness even in heavenly victory. His honoring of his own woundedness makes it safe for us not only to be wounded but to recognize our woundedness as part of what makes us blessed.

But too many of us live our brokenness under a curse rather than under the blessing of God. Henri Nouwen says, "Living our brokenness under the curse means that we experience our pain as a confirmation of our negative feelings about ourselves. It is like saying, 'I always suspected that I was useless or worthless, and now I am sure of it because of what is happening to me'"[6] Too often our poverty feeds our self-rejection, because the false self will interpret pain as proof of our defectiveness and use it as part of the ongoing indictment against the incompetent self. And such "brokenness" serves as an exemption from kingdom work rather than the means to it. Brokenness is never recognized as the powerlessness that empowers, as that which drives us to the feet of our merciful Jesus.

God calls us, says Nouwen, to pull our brokenness from the darkness of the curse, from the false self's misinterpretations, and into the light of God's blessing. To do so requires a shift in how reality is deciphered. It means giving up our judgments about success and failure, resisting the urge to fashion those judgments into a club with which to beat ourselves or others. But more than this, it means to change how we see. When brokenness is brought under the blessing, it becomes "an opportunity to purify and deepen the blessing that rests upon us."[7] What does this mean? Brokenness as blessing enables us to see reality differently and to confront how we view pain and suffering.

Competition says pain and suffering are never success. We equate pain with some misstep. Suffering is evidence of our defectiveness or is payback for our sins. This was certainly true in Jesus' day, when maladies and calamities were considered the effects of someone's sin. The disciples asked Jesus, "Rabbi, who sinned, this man or his parents, that he was born blind?" (John 9:2). Jesus' response correctly labels reality and should be an encouragement to us all: "This happened so that the work of God might be displayed in his life" (v. 3). Dare we believe this about our own pain and weakness? Can we see suffering as a place of potential blessing?

Like it or not, suffering is a necessary part of holiness. This statement is not intended to minimize real hurt and terrible agony, nor to paint a happy face on people as they grapple with these things. But suffering can be more than just pain, and distress can have meaning greater than itself. One writer puts it this way: "In the reckonings of humans, suffering is a disqualification for life: in the ways of God it is an equipment for life."[8] Our painful moments can become a crucible through which Christ-in-us is formed. Rather than evidence of a failed relationship with God, pain can deepen relationship by revealing God from new angles.

Like the disciples, we have trouble finding the blessing of God in suffering, especially in the pain that ushers from it. Gerald May talks about an unfortunate trend he calls the "happiness mentality": "The basic assumption of the happiness mentality . . . is that if one lives one's life correctly one will be happy. The corollary of this assumption is that if one is not happy, one is doing something wrong. . . . Many people now feel any sign of unhappiness in their lives is a symptom of psychological or spiritual disorder."[9] Even if we accept the value of suffering, we might balk when it comes to living with the emotional states that come with our pain. Within many of our faith communities, it is unsafe to admit heavy feelings. We see painful emotions—depression, confusion, doubt, and hopelessness—as evidence that ours is not a strong or authentic faith. But desolate feelings are part of our insufficiency and weakness and, therefore, part of our brokenness. Nouwen says, "Joy and sorrow are the parents of our spiritual growth."[10] Joy and sorrow—each grounds the other.

Paul, in the same epistle where he declared that Christ's power is made perfect in weakness, plainly owned his pain and suffering in ministry as well as his brokenness: "We were under great pressure, far beyond our ability to endure, so that we despaired even of life. Indeed, in our hearts we felt the sentence of death" (2 Cor. 1:8–9). Then he expresses that such suffering has meaning, keeping us dependent upon the Lord: "But this happened that we might not rely on ourselves but on God, who raises the dead. He has delivered us from such a deadly peril, and he will deliver us. On him we have set our hope that he will continue to deliver us" (vv. 9–10).

Knowing God in Our Blessed Brokenness

In chapter 3, I shared the story of Jim, a pastor who experienced destruction caused by false-self believers, driven by power, within his church. Up to that point, Jim had led a relatively unwounded life. But his experience with the collapse of the church—and himself—changed everything, including how he experienced and related to God.

During the dismantling of the church, Jim focused all of his energies on keeping the congregation going, confronting inappropriate people, and trying to hold his staff and himself together. In the middle of the strife, everything felt threatened, even his relationship with the Lord: "Having God as your boss is intimidating. Not only was I losing the world I was given to oversee, but I felt that the person who was my boss was against me as well. What I discovered in that place was a complete emptiness."

Jim's breaking point came one morning when he rose and showered. He toweled off and, without dressing, laid on his bed and stared at the ceiling. Devastated in every way—physically, emotionally, spiritually—Jim's nakedness was a picture of his whole life. He remembers that moment: "I was at the end of myself, in a downward free fall, and I threw myself on the

bed and said, 'This is it, this is all there is of me, just flesh. I
have nothing left to offer you, God, nothing left to give you. All
I can do is just be here, just as I am.'" At that moment, Jim
surrendered, realizing that his efforts weren't going to save the
church or anyone else. Jesus was the only hope he had. Lying
on the bed that morning, Jim came fully present to his own
brokenness and to God. Through his brokenness, he came to
truly know God.

Jim says, "There's a sense in which you can know about the
love of God and never be touched personally by the love of
God." That had been his life. But within the experience of his
brokenness, Jim, a person raised by godly parents and a minister of the gospel for twenty years, finally came to truly know,
finally came to experience, the love of God. "The love of God
was a theological concept that had not become personal reality," Jim recalls. "I could say all the right things about God and
know the theological concepts and quote the verses and appropriate that as a reality. But I had not found the place of personal receptivity to the love of God until I was broken and was
just lying there. Brokenness is the in-breaking place for the
love of God." The results of Jim's breaking were immense love
and inexplicable joy. God guided him through the rubble of
his church plant and his own mistaken notions about God and
himself, and Jim continues to minister to a new congregation
in powerful and significant ways.

Have you ever experienced receptivity to God in your brokenness? It's like taking a step into thin air. You come to the
end of yourself and say, "I can't do it anymore," awaiting the
blow from God that never comes. Miraculously, you are held
safe. Like a baby bird cupped in the hands of God, you understand beyond cognition what the love of God really is. If you've
never experienced your brokenness as blessing, as drawing you
deeper into Christ to heal the schism between head and heart,
then you don't truly know God beyond hearsay.

And as God's love is received and the true self emerges, the
idol created by the false self crumbles, and we realize, maybe

for the first time, who God is. For it is in brokenness that we most perfectly come to know God. Is this a startling statement? To commune with God other than from the ground of our smallness, our weakness, our woundedness, even our nothingness, is to relate from a place tainted by the myth of competence and our illusory strengths. Only in deep poverty can we most fully apprehend, with both head and heart, the person of God. There is no other way to know God except by receiving his love and mercy unconditionally. Any knowledge of God apart from our brokenness is largely derivative.

God's love is bigger and better than we were ever told. The truth is, our brokenness is at the heart of kingdom life because the power of Christ is most perfectly expressed within our weakness. Merton's words forever changed my view of brokenness:

> If we know how great is the love of Jesus for us we will never be afraid to go to Him in all our poverty, all our weakness, all our spiritual wretchedness and infirmity. Indeed, when we understand the true nature of His love for us, we will prefer to come to Him poor and helpless. We will never be ashamed of our distress. Distress is to our advantage when we have nothing to seek but mercy. . . . *The surest sign that we have received a spiritual understanding of God's love for us is the appreciation of our own poverty in the light of His infinite mercy.* (italics added)[11]

The best gauge of how intimately you understand God and his kingdom lies in your response to your brokenness. In fact, in light of Jesus, the suffering servant, it's evident that God *prefers* to be known through poverty. This is the way of Jesus, our God who was broken, who blesses and empowers us.

Owned Brokenness and Empowered Ministry

My friend Abby is a multitalented, educated, highly intelligent woman. She has poised speaking skills, great talents in singing, songwriting, and piano, and a zeal for biblical truth. We enjoy talking together about the things of God. On one occasion we discussed her longing for God to use her talents in ways that would build the kingdom. But our conversation about talents and the kingdom that day set my soul awry. I felt God intersecting our conversation, and I said to her, "Abby, you have all these gifts—God has given you much—but the deepest ministry you'll ever enter into will flow from your brokenness, not your talents, which are illusory at best anyway." In response, her facial expression resembled a deer caught in the headlights. She was clearly wrestling with my words.

One of the glories of the kingdom is this: When we own our brokenness and make it entirely available to the Lord, our wounds and weakness are transformed into windows—windows through which we and others can see God more clearly and thereby praise him with greater might. Living in brokenness keeps us dependent upon God, and there we await his power, his wisdom, and his love to minister through us. Kneeling at the feet of Jesus—dependent, broken—we reach out to the weak and wounded who surround us. This is the posture of the most powerful ministry we will ever enter into.

The time I spent with Abby that day seemed a foreshadow. Not long after, Abby acutely experienced her brokenness, leading to a period of clinical depression and counseling. With the Lord's help, she went through her own valley of the shadow and emerged with a deepened faith and widened ministry. She still uses her talents for God, but her ministry now possesses a different quality, a more tender mercy, a deeper presence and godly power.

What I said to Abby during that conversation long ago is true for all of us. Our deepest ministry, our most compassionate acts, our most Jesus-like service, emerges from the wounds and weakness that have met the balm of Christ. Brokenness is not at odds with service for Christ; indeed, owned brokenness is the key to empowered ministry. We can barely believe this. Yet we must become convinced of the paradox Paul experienced: "My power is made perfect in weakness." Some of us think that our histories are too torn, too traumatic, and that we are too weak to be of use in the kingdom. But to such believers God declares, "Blessed are you!" We who are torn and weak are the people who live the literal definition of compassion—*cum patior,* "to suffer with"—because we are not in denial about our poverty. It is to the weak that the good news of the kingdom comes, first to the broken, then to a wounded world.

Years ago, Jean attended a Christian college in the Midwest. The student who lived next door to her in the dormitory was a typical church girl—a quiet and conservative freshman who exuded sweetness and innocence. With a background marked by abuse and abandonment, Jean had difficulty relating to Sue. One evening, however, Jean heard sobbing coming from the next room. She stepped into the hallway where Sue's roommate told her that Sue had just revealed that she had been sexually abused as a child.

"What did you say to her?" asked Jean.

"I didn't know what to say," the roommate replied.

Jean didn't hesitate. "Well, she needs to talk to someone who's been there," and she knocked on Sue's door. Jean's own journey of brokenness and her commitment to restoration empowered her to minister to Sue. Suddenly these two women who had nothing in common had everything in common. Jean spent a long time ministering to Sue and later helped her find the resources for healing. Looking back on the incident, Jean says, "I knew she needed to talk to me. It gave me a window of opportunity to be Jesus with skin on."

In our brokenness, we become Jesus with skin on, making God's work within us available to others and fulfilling the words of Isaiah: "He has sent me to bind up the brokenhearted, to proclaim freedom for the captives and release from darkness for the prisoners . . . to comfort all who mourn, and provide for those who grieve in Zion" (61:1–3). Some of us, though, desire to be a comforter, binding up the brokenhearted—but through the false self. We want to comfort the broken while refusing to be broken, unwilling to be brought, begging, to the feet of Jesus. But Isaiah says that the ones who have received ministry in their deep neediness become the "oaks of righteousness," ministers of God who renew and restore our devastated world (vv. 3–6). Without owning our brokenness, ministry can only be done from a position of power, a drive of the false self.

To truly be Jesus with skin on, we must first deal with our own poverty, our own powerlessness, our own brokenness. Reading the story of Jean and Sue, you no doubt felt sorry about the abuse Sue suffered and were glad that Jean was around to identify with her and help her. "But," you might say, "that's far from my story. I'm not really wounded, so I can't be expected to minister out of brokenness." True, you may have managed to live without major wounding, but poverty is not simply a specific event; it's part and parcel of the human condition. Everyone is impoverished, but some of us deny our weakness and woundedness. In doing so, we display a shallow view of sin, and we resist embracing our weaknesses and limitations.

Can you recognize the darkness, the waywardness, the secret and evil intents of your thought life, and the sin clinging to your heart? If we're honest, all of us experience the shame, the frustration, and the sense of smallness in knowing that our best, most polished efforts to love God and to love people always fall short. We must declare—and own—our fracturedness, our insufficiency, as does the apostle Paul: "I do not understand what I do. For what I want to do I do not do, but what I hate I do. . . . As it is, it is no longer I myself who do it, but it is sin living in me. I know that nothing good lives in me, that is, in my sinful nature. For I have the desire to do what is good, but I cannot carry it out" (Rom. 7:15–18). If you've never experienced brokenness over your incompleteness, your weaknesses, your sin that wounds others and tears at your own soul, then you'll never minister profoundly to others or delve deeply into the heart of Jesus Christ. If you believe yourself to be unimpoverished and, therefore, absolved from brokenness, then you are living a religious fantasy.

A year ago, I visited Abbey in the city where she now lives.

She played for me a videotape of her testimony in the church where she is involved in youth, women's, and music ministries. On the screen I watched this beautiful and transparent woman speaking. She could have displayed her musical talents or biblical knowledge, but she didn't. She talked about her ongoing struggle with depression, breaking into tears at times, and how God was meeting her and restoring her. She told me that the aftermath of her saying out loud what many in that congregation struggled with silently was significant. Many came to her with their own stories of depression lived in shame. Reflecting on what it means for her to minister out of her brokenness, Abbey says, "I have no more illusions that I have it together. I'm no longer above people, benevolently helping them. I can empathize on their level. Before my depression, I don't think I could tell the difference between true-self and false-self ministry. When I'm in my true self, that's the self that's truly broken and can't minister without God. In order to have the freedom to minister anymore, I have to be aware of my brokenness. If I'm not owning my brokenness on a day-to-day basis, I'm ineffective as a Christian and as a minister. Period."

Grace and Wholeness in the Kingdom

Grace is an overused word. It gets tossed around in sermons, books, and Bible studies. But full, abundant grace is a rarity in most churches. Preachers and teachers argue, encourage, cajole, and even try to shame believers into becoming people of grace. What most call for is simply a type of conduct: give grace, show mercy, even if you haven't received it. So believers go about doing the "grace thing," cranking out appropriate behaviors. We were created to live in a kingdom filled with mercy, forgiveness, and the power to live godly lives—a kingdom of grace. But, when we attempt to reach and to serve an impoverished world with our paltry, humanized versions of grace, we're left in wide-eyed wonder at the frequent inability of the church to make the Good News look and sound like good news.

Grace is the meaning of the gospel, the great mystery of our salvation, and the glory of our relationship with God. It's also the crux of an empowered ministry. We all know grace is central, but we find it elusive. Yet, the kingdom truth for nurturing a life of grace is not difficult: allow yourself to become a broken person. The only people of authentic grace in this world are broken people. Our capacity to receive grace is directly proportional to the degree to which we own our brokenness. Returning to 2 Corinthians 12, we see that grace and weakness are fused in the Lord's response to Paul about his thorn: "My grace is sufficient for you, for my power is made perfect in weakness" (v. 9). Grace is made for the weakness and woundedness of humanity. If we refuse to embrace our poverty and own our brokenness—the very place for which the salve of God's grace was created—how can we say we understand and receive grace? And how can we possibly offer it to others?

But receiving grace depends upon our willingness to own our brokenness. Jesus' parable in Matthew 18—the servant who owed the king ten thousand talents—depicts our dilemma of receiving and giving grace. Ten thousand talents symbolizes a completely unattainable amount of money, and the servant had no chance of ever raising such funds. Out of mercy, the king extended grace by forgiving the debt. But we all know the story—the servant then left the king's presence and five minutes later had an acquaintance imprisoned because he couldn't repay a minuscule amount of money. Why couldn't the servant extend mercy in light of the extravagant mercy freely bestowed to him? Why couldn't the servant respond with grace?

The answer lies in his response to the king: "Be patient with me, . . . and I will pay back everything" (Matt. 18:26). The servant never asked for mercy because he didn't believe he needed it. This man had not come to the end of himself and his ability to repay. He was lost in the illusion that he could eventually pay back his unimaginable debt by lining up the right amount of moneymaking behaviors. He wasn't broken. The servant allowed the debt to be erased, but he still believed that he could repay it if he had to. Grace in the form of the king's mercy was extended, but only superficially received, so naturally the servant had no mercy, no form of grace, to extend to anyone else.[12]

We can clearly see how foolish the servant was, but isn't this parable played out a million times over in our churches every day? Is it not the story of most of us who say we follow Jesus; is it not your story and mine? We take in the grace of God superficially, saying we need grace, but spending our days on a treadmill of performance, doing everything we can to be "good enough" so that the debt might be paid back or at least the balance due reduced. We receive our King's grace but only enough for our tickets to heaven. We never let grace enter farther than the doorstep of our hearts, because owning our brokenness feels too risky, too frightening, too costly. We take Jesus' maxim "blessed are the poor in spirit"—and the Greek is highly emphatic here, "for *theirs alone* is the kingdom of heaven"[13]—and decide that it's only relevant for two minutes at the time of conversion. We then go about the business of manufacturing more right behaviors while Jesus—the broken, wound-bearing Christ—weeps tears we refuse to see, or are too afraid to touch, on the faces of our poor-in-spirit brothers and sisters.

Grace refused becomes mercy withheld. Let us not wonder at the close of the parable where the king confronts the unmerciful servant: "'Shouldn't you have had mercy on your fellow servant just as I had on you?' In anger his master turned him over to the jailers to be tortured, until he should pay back all he owed" (Matt. 18:33–34). The servant failed to recognize that the king's extension of mercy and forgiveness—the stuff of grace—needed to be replicated in his own life. And this failure occurred because he was never truly present to his debt—never allowing himself to be crushed beneath the intolerable weight of it, never letting it break him.

We must recognize our own debts, the millions we owe, the unimaginable sum that we can never repay. We must embrace our insufficiency, our weakness, in the presence of the love and grace extended by a holy God. Admitting such brokenness shatters our myth of competence, but this shattering is like that of the alabaster jar at the feet of Jesus—it perfumes the whole house with the sweet aroma of wholehearted devotion, a grace fully received. This is salvation, true and complete.

And out of receiving the love of God—receiving it in fact, not just theory—and deeply encountering the grace of God comes wholeness. Wholeness is ours—*now*—because in our brokenness, Jesus completes us. Wholeness is not the absence of wounds but the fullness of Christ within our woundedness. When we consent to own and to live out of our brokenness, we resonate with Brennan Manning's words: "Wholeness is brokenness owned and thereby healed."[14]

We can live a life not based on what we generate but on what we receive. Jesus really does complete us. The Good News really is better than we ever imagined. In the kingdom, we can call our brokenness blessed and cherish it as the place where we most intimately know God and ourselves.

Brothers and sisters, poverty is the only door into grace and freedom. Do we need any greater reason to rejoice in our insufficiency? We can, to use Leanne Payne's phrase, celebrate our smallness because our God reigns and his arm is strong to save and uphold us. And with the apostle Paul, we are able to "boast all the more gladly" in our weaknesses. Manning provides the best benediction to those of us who have tasted the freedom and goodness of coming to the end of ourselves, of celebrating our blessed brokenness, and of becoming an ever-emerging scent of grace in a fallen world:

> May all your expectations be frustrated.
> May all your plans be thwarted.
> May all your desires wither to nothingness,
> that you may experience
> the powerlessness and poverty of a child
> and sing and dance in the love of God
> who is Father, Son, and Holy Spirit.
>   Amen.

7

DISCIPLINES OF THE TRUE SELF

Love and Contemplation

So we fix our eyes not on what is seen, but on what is unseen.
For what is seen is temporary, but what is unseen is eternal.
—Paul the Apostle (2 Corinthians 4:18)

Contemplative prayer is a way of awakening to the reality in
which we are immersed. We rarely think of the air we breathe,
yet it is in us and around us all the time. In similar fashion, the
presence of God penetrates us, is all around us, is always
embracing us. Our awareness, unfortunately, is not awake to
that dimension of reality. The purpose of prayer, the sacraments,
and spiritual disciplines is to awaken us.
—Thomas Keating

If we are designed to be in communion with God, if God is our
Lover, then we have to indulge in the things that lovers do. The
lover wishes always to be in the loved one's presence, and to gaze
and to hold. The name for this loving regard is contemplation.
—Alan Jones

In his book, *The Divine Conspiracy,* Dallas Willard discusses "bar-code faith": "Think of the bar codes now used on goods in most stores. The scanner responds only to the bar code. It makes no difference what is in the bottle or package that bears it, or whether the sticker is on the 'right' one or not. The calculator responds through its electronic eye to the bar code and totally disregards everything else. If the ice cream sticker is on the dog food, the dog food is ice cream, so far as the scanner knows or cares."[1]

The bar-code image represents much of contemporary Christendom—a onetime salvation experience applies our bar codes, which tell God and humanity that we're forgiven sinners and heaven-bound. We don't have to change or be transformed. Our future is assured. It doesn't matter what's inside the package, because when we're slid over the great scanner in the sky, God will see the "saved" bar code, and we're in.

The truth of this analogy is evident in how we approach spiritual disciplines and discipleship. The emphasis in Christian culture is too much upon doing the disciplines as an activity rather than upon the spiritual transformation they are meant to effect. By and large, our discipleship "program" is to hand out Bibles, tell people to study and pray, and leave them to their own devices. A few take these practices seriously, but the majority either don't engage in regular spiritual disciplines or do so with little effect.

Meister Eckhart, a thirteenth-century writer, said, "There are plenty to follow our Lord halfway but not the other half." The disciplines, and the spirituality that surrounds them, determine if ours will be a secondhalf discipleship or instead something half-hearted. Second-half discipleship requires a radical renaissance of how we view disciplines and how we enter into them.

Willard describes what a spiritual discipline is: "A discipline for the spiritual life is . . . nothing but an activity undertaken to bring us into more effective cooperation with Christ and his Kingdom."[2] Richard Foster adds, "God has given us the Disciplines of the spiritual life as a means of receiving His grace.

The Disciplines allow us to place ourselves before God so that He can transform us."[3] Core disciplines center around prayer and Bible reading but also include practices such as silence and solitude, fasting, giving, worship, and more. The purpose of spiritual disciplines is that we more and more exhibit the fruit of the Spirit in our lives (love, joy, peace, patience, kindness, goodness, faithfulness, gentleness, and self-control) and love God in all of our living. While this description sounds good, is it in most cases reality? If not, what is our reality surrounding spiritual disciplines?

The Disciplines: How We Picture Them

Imagine a beautiful summer day at the ballpark. The infield tosses the ball around. The pitcher warms up, drilling the ball into the catcher's mitt. The batters take practice swings. The game is ready to begin. The teams, inning by inning, demonstrate their preparation with graceful movements, from hitting line drives to snagging them in leather gloves. Many batters strike out while one or two hit a home run. Preparation determines how well the players perform on the field.

The scene just described one of the most popular metaphors used for spiritual disciplines. The associations are obvious: You can't hit the ball out of the park if you don't prepare for the game. The cause and effect between training and performance is abundantly clear. Similarly, the spiritual disciplines constitute Christian training for kingdom life and kingdom work. Paul uses the athletic metaphor to talk about readiness for spiritual gain: "Do you not know that in a race all the runners run, but only one gets the prize? Run in such a way as to get the prize. Everyone who competes in the games goes into strict training. They do it to get a crown that will not last; but we do it to get a crown that will last forever" (1 Cor. 9:24–25). To get the crown that does not perish, we're told, we must work and work diligently.

Honestly, I'm attracted to this metaphor. It's tangible to me

and explains the importance of entering into the disciplines.
And through the years, I've accepted this metaphor as the way
to picture spiritual practices. As the baseball player is concerned
with right technique—batting stance or pitching into the strike
zone—we Christians exert ourselves, focusing our energies on
our spiritual version of fielding grounders. When asked, "Why
do you do the disciplines?" the answer is "So, I can perform
well for the kingdom." But, as discussed in chapter 4, a focus
on performance alone can be debilitating. If improved performance is our only way to understand the disciplines, we can
easily fall into error.

We may drag ourselves to our Bibles and prayer times, and
once there, be secretly glad for any little diversion. We use
accountability groups to ensure that we keep up with our disciplines and daily quiet times. And even this behavior is in the
minority; most of us make excuses for not doing these spiritual
activities. Is this how it's supposed to be? True, for newer or
younger Christians, especially for we who grew up in the church,
disciplines-as-obligation can be accepted as part of early formation. But the majority of us never move on. I can't help but
wonder if we're not anchored within the sports metaphor, where
an emphasis on performance and drills has proven insufficient
to open for us the glories of the kingdom.

The athletic metaphor helps frame and give structure to how
we approach the disciplines, but this metaphor must not be
the heart of how we engage with the disciplines. We need a
counterbalancing metaphor for entering into a fresh understanding of spiritual practices. We need courtship.

The spiritual disciplines are the ground of holy friendship,
where God pours his love and mercy into our hearts, enliven-
ing the eternal soul within. The disciplines are also the marriage bed, the place where we consummate God's spiritual
courtship: "My lover is mine and I am his" (Song 2:16). They
express the heart of Jesus' last prayer for us in John: "That the
love you have for me may be in them and that I myself may be
in them" (17:26). The metaphor of the marriage union is po-

tent in both the Old and New Testaments, from God's faithful betrothal to harlot Israel, to Jesus as our bridegroom. The disciplines must contain an element of order and exertion, but if they are not also the place of spousal union, then there is no romance—only rigor. The ballplayer metaphor stresses action— initiate, strive, perform. But the disciplines are an invitation to yield, to give ourselves over, to receive. They invite us into relationship and into intimacy.

As God woos us toward union, he says, "In that day . . . you will call me 'my husband'; you will no longer call me 'my master'" (Hos. 2:16). This powerful portrait of love needs to shape our life within the disciplines. When the question is then asked, "Why do you do the disciplines?" the answer will be "I belong to my lover, and his desire is for me" (Song 7:10). The marriage metaphor raises the stakes higher: God doesn't just want me to show up and perform; something deeper and riskier is required, something passionate and wild is occurring at the deepest level of my being.

True-self living hinges upon how we do the disciplines. And for the vast majority of Christians, the charts for navigating the spiritual disciplines come almost exclusively from the false self. The ways we approach and utilize the disciplines tend to reinforce the false self. If being the beloved constitutes our real identity, our eternal true self, and if love really is the currency of the kingdom, then when approaching the disciplines, we must find the passion of the marriage bed that calls us into second-half discipleship.

Distorted Spirituality of the Disciplines

If I'm a ballplayer in the athletic metaphor of the disciplines, I'm concerned with improvement in my play. "How am I performing?" is an all-important question, since that's the aim of my training. Transferred to the spiritual realm, such an attitude is disastrous.

The center of this false-self approach to spiritual disciplines is measurement. We think of our spiritual practices in terms of things we can quantify—time, insights, intensity—and in terms of product—our maturity, our sense of invulnerability, our amassed wisdom. This tendency is the fallout of the myth of competence, in which improvement helps us gain a sense of mastery. When the false self is in charge, the disciplines, as well as the life that surrounds them, must stand against a spiritual yardstick. Our safety and satisfaction comes when the yardstick yields a marked "increase." We note how long we study the Bible and pray, judging how well it went by how we feel, or what we gleaned, or whether or not there's a product to show for our efforts. Thus, the barometer of our spirituality is gauged by superficial behaviors and responses. And if our performance is a success, we feel good about our spirituality; if we fail—and most people see themselves as failures at doing the disciplines—we become entrenched in guilt, having let God down.

If measuring and producing, then, become the goal, we don't so much want to pray to God as we want to pray to God without distractions, or with intense fervency, or whatever else. We don't want to be with God as much as we want an emotionally tangible experience of God—peace, passion, comfort. We don't read the Bible to simply soak in the Word but read for the trophy of luminous insights or to plow through so many chapters. We don't want the holy life the disciplines lead us to so much as we want a life wherein we feel wise, useful, and entirely put together.

We, then, obsess about our spiritual growth. The big question is, "How am I doing with God?" and we search the mall directory of our spiritual lives, looking for the "You Are Here" arrow. But, in fact, the moment we ask ourselves, "How am I doing with God?" and start mapping out our progress, we're automatically not doing very well; we've taken our eyes off of God and put them on self—and the false self at that. We cannot measure and judge our spiritual growth and adore Jesus in the same moment.

In a sense, your spiritual growth is none of your business. Calculating the effects of your disciplines and your discipleship is not your concern. Our ideas of growth easily become something we look to, other than God, to find security, worth, power, and approval—the drives of the false self. Should we notice when the Spirit's fruit is either absent or abundant? Certainly, but that's the bulk of what we should do: notice and then submit ourselves to God either way. Our journey in the Spirit is not about yardsticks, spiritual levels, or competitive comparisons. Such things will surely thwart the work of God. Basil Pennington reminds us that "growth in the Christian life is a matter of intensification, of growing toward loving God in Christ with one's *whole* mind, *whole* heart, *whole* soul, and *whole* strength.[4]

If the false self reigns so much within and around the disciplines, then how can we move toward a life that is truly founded and flavored by Christ-in-me? Thomas Merton has described society as a shipwreck from which every person must swim for his or her life, and in many aspects, this is no less true for Christian society. If the true self's lifeblood flows from the disciplines, we must cultivate practices that will not simply placate the false self. We need disciplines that by their very nature open us to the presence of God and to receiving his love. We need a countercultural response.

When exploring the disciplines amidst the pulls of false self, how can we exchange the ballplayer for the beloved? There is a path that averts many of the subtle evils of culture, a path that brings us to the marriage bed, opening the receptivity and the wonder of the human soul. One reasonable response to the shipwreck of Christian culture's approach to the disciplines is to become contemplatives within the culture.

What Is Contemplative Spirituality?

Many of us associate the word *contemplative* with convents and monasteries, places filled with hooded figures who spend most of their days praying to God and chanting on the way to lunch. It feels very unlike our own lives, crowded with rush and activity. Perhaps we'd like a slower life, one that contemplates

God more, but how do we reconcile silence and solitude with laptops and cell phones? Contemplative spirituality is not, however, about a place or specific faith heritage. It's about opening to certain disciplines and a call to a certain way of being.

Two primary principles help to understand contemplative spirituality.[5] First, that God is the foundation and preeminent author of creation, sustaining all things. We need not worry about "getting somewhere" or about striving to "get to God." Contemplative spirituality assumes with both head and heart, meaning within theology *and* actual practice, that if I am in Christ, God is already fully present. Because of our fallenness, however, we fail to walk in the light of this reality. Thus, the second principle of contemplative spirituality is that the purpose of our disciplines is to become present to God. Being present to God is not just having ideas about him but soaking in God's love and mercy for us as our sole means of transformation and carrying that Presence, that love, into our day.

As contemplatives within the culture, as true-self-emerging persons, we stand distinct from the culture, in it but not of it. And distinguishing ourselves from the culture is not a passive thing. It is not sufficient to simply abstain from certain activities; we must endeavor to embrace something other, consent to become something other. Larry Crabb delineates contemplative spirituality, distinguishing between two types of people within our faith communities—mystics and managers. Managers "stop with head knowledge of the gospel" while a mystic experiences "the felt arousal of spiritual passions within the regenerate heart, passions that can have no existence apart from a Spirit-revealed knowledge of truth and the prompting of the same Spirit to enjoy that truth."[6] The mystic life is dominated by an insatiable hunger for God. A. W. Tozer speaks of what it is to be a mystic in our evangelical context:

> The word "mystic" . . . refers to that personal spiritual experience common to the saints of Bible times and well known to multitudes of persons in the post-Biblical

era. I refer to the evangelical mystic who has been brought by the gospel into intimate fellowship with the Godhead. His theology is no less and no more than is taught in the Christian Scriptures. . . . *He differs from the ordinary orthodox Christian only because he experiences his faith down in the depths of his sentient being while the other does not.* He exists in a world of spiritual reality. He is quietly, deeply, and sometimes almost ecstatically aware of the Presence of God in his own nature and in the world around him. His religious experience is something elemental, as old as time and the creation. It is immediate acquaintance with God by union with the Eternal Son. It is to know that which passes knowledge. (italics added)[7]

In the way of the mystic, head and heart become integrated, and life becomes immersed in the presence of God. This is the zenith of contemplative spirituality. The Lord is both known and experienced as a normative part of Christian living. And the point is not only to know or to experience God but for such knowledge and experience to open more of our lives to worshipful living.

This kind of integrated living *is* within our reach. Contemplation, as the word indicates, contemplates something—the person of God—not in lively mental interaction but in the restful manner that two lovers abide in each other's presence. Contemplation, then, is a love-filled, spirit-to-Spirit gazing. Our right thoughts about God—accurate theology—are vital, of course, but they are meant to be the starting gate of kingdom life, not the finish line.

But we assume that our thoughts about God and his truth *are* the finish line in our devotional lives. Our culture's overestimation of the intellect tells us that truthful thoughts are an end in themselves. They are not. By themselves, thoughts—no matter how good or right—are intended to be a means and only contain eternal significance as they compel us into the presence of God. After all, what is the point of having right thoughts or dialogue about God if they do not lead us deeper into God? We stop too soon. We are too much spiritual materialists, too pleased with the more obvious manifestations of our relationship with God, such as insights and ideas.

What, then, is the end of our disciplines? Is it only to form correct thoughts about God or to deepen our awareness of God himself? Is it to live more fully in his presence, loving him and worshiping him with our whole hearts? If the aim of disciplines is awareness of God's presence and love, then contemplation must be legitimate, for contemplation is a path whereby we might place ourselves before God, experiencing him, loving him, surrendering in worship to his will. The anonymous author of *The Cloud of Unknowing*, a spiritual guidebook written to a Christian community during the fourteenth century, helps us to understand the good but limiting work of forming thoughts about God:

> A man may know completely and ponder thoroughly every created thing and its works, yes, and God's works too, but not God himself. Thought cannot comprehend God. And so I prefer to abandon all I can know, choosing rather to love him whom I cannot know. Though we cannot know him we can love him. By love he may be touched and embraced, never by thought. Of course, we do well at times to ponder God's majesty or kindness for the insight these meditations may bring. But in the real contemplative work you must set all this aside.[8]

Here we encounter the one great principle of contemplation—the primacy of love. Right thoughts about God have wonderful merit but only as they lead us into the heart of God, plunging us ever deeper into the love of God. And this is a love we can *know,* not just know about, and we may come to know it now through both specific spiritual practices and in how we approach these practices. Any spiritual practice that brings us into restful awareness of God as the reality in which we are constantly immersed can be called contemplative. But to further explore the way of the contemplative mystic, two specific practices are discussed below.

The Discipline of *Lectio Divina*

Joanne was a stay-at-home mom in her thirties who was experiencing postpartum depression after the birth of her third child. Her relationship with God felt distant and dry. The busyness and stress of a new baby and her spiritual desert created a different kind of hunger within Joanne. She says of that time, "I had an inner longing to figure out what prayer was, and the pat, churchy answers were more formulaic than relationship-based. They just didn't work for me. Instead of being fed the classical spiritual disciplines, I was told ten things to do at five in the morning. My relationship with God was more about lists than about conversation."

The turning point for Joanne came when a woman spoke to her mom's group about disciplines that were relationally oriented, grounded in being, not just doing. Joanne, then, began to meditate upon Scripture, to enter into quiet prayer, and to learn about the spiritual value of silence and solitude. She read books on approaching the disciplines in more intimate ways, saying, "I discovered there were a wealth of people who had what I wanted and had been experiencing these things for centuries."

Joanne is not alone in her search for practices that aren't about checking items off a spiritual to-do list. Many of us resonate with her longing for disciplines that create intimate conversation with our Beloved. One of those classical disciplines that Joanne embraced was *lectio divina*—Latin for "divine" or "sacred reading." Dating back to the early Christian centuries, *lectio divina* is an ancient way of prayerfully listening to, and engaging with, the Holy Scriptures.

My approach incorporates the four traditional movements

of *lectio divina*. These movements naturally flow into each other through prayerful reading. The practical suggestions I include with each movement are simply one way to structure the time of *lectio divina*. Even though these movements might seem rather involved at first glance, the process is simple and need not be time consuming. Even five minutes is enough to practice *lectio divina*.

1. Lectio: Taking Up the Scripture

In this first movement, simply take up the Word of God and read. But it's really not that simple because Bible reading for most Christians is on a par with eating a plate full of bland vegetables. We know they're good for us, so we grin and swallow them. But there's little joy or life there.

When we approach reading the Bible, we often do so with the unspoken assumption that the Bible is lifeless. In reality, we are the lifeless ones. Our Bible reading lacks life because we fail to listen with the ear of the heart, a disposition of willingness, of holy listening, that changes how we come to the Bible. Henri Nouwen explains the difference between typical reading and spiritual reading. They should be approached differently, but we have little idea what spiritual reading really is:

> Most of us read to acquire knowledge or to satisfy our curiosity. When we want to know how to repair a car, cook a meal, build a house, help a handicapped person, give a lecture, etc., we have to do a certain amount of reading. When we want to keep informed about world news, sports news, entertainment news, and society news, we must turn to different newspapers and magazines. The purpose of spiritual reading, however, is not to master knowledge or information, but to let God's Spirit master us. Strange as it may sound, spiritual reading means to let ourselves be read by God![9]

The posture with which we approach the Bible matters greatly. When we read the Bible (or other literature we sense God might speak through), we read not for information but for transformation. For me, this means reading slowly and attentively, aware of my reactions to the text and aware that Jesus is reading along with me. I stop when something catches my interest or pierces my consciousness. The *lectio* movement understands that the value of reading the Bible lies not in the activity itself but in the degree to which I am opened to God, changed by the Word, and transformed to do his will. For this end, a purely head-centered, intellectual posture only gets me halfway there. To truly read spiritually, I must enter the heart's path of experiential listening, resting, and receiving.

My time of reading begins with an acknowledgment of God's love for me. I take up the Word of God, understanding that while the Bible is certainly my guide for obedience and holiness, it is also a long love letter from home. It is the Word from my Beloved, and to never read it as such is to read it without full benefit. Love is the key to understanding Scripture as deep calling to deep—God's love held out to me and my response of love. On this point, one author says, "The criterion by which Christ still assesses his friends and repudiators is 'Do you love me?' What do we make of the Bible if we forget this, even if we hold to everything else?"[10] In this attitude, I expect communion, not just communication. The point is not to get to the end of a particular passage but to open my full awareness, my full person, to God and to sit like Mary—listening, adoring—at the feet of Jesus.

So, as you do the *lectio* movement, read your chosen passage, drink in the text, receive what is in the Scripture while listening for a word, phrase, or sentence that catches your attention. Rest a few moments with whatever arises, repeating the words silently, while pondering them. Rest and silence throughout this practice are vital. In rest and silence, we are more disposed to hearing and to responding.

Come to the Word of God without expectations, save Jesus'

promise that when you ask for bread you will not be given a
stone. Few things can corrupt a time of prayerful reading like
specific expectations about what you need God to do for you.
Such expectations subtly assert themselves as your focal point.
Instead, simply believe, as the child that you are, that your Father sits next to you and longs to share this little space of time
with you. That spiritual reality is more comforting and more
remarkable than any other gift God might bring.

2. Meditatio: Engaging with the Passage

Now that you know where the passage is going, read it again
in a meditative way. Our contemporary definition of meditation refers to some sort of quiet, transcendent state, but that is
not the case here. Meditation involves the active engagement
with the passage, using both your imagination and intellect.
What images come to mind for you around the Scripture? What
questions do you have about the passage? What insights or connections within the text do you notice? Is there something you
want to know more about?

The *meditatio* movement culminates as, in an attitude of
prayer, you ask God how the passage might link to your own
life: "Lord, what are you pointing at for me in this passage?"
"How is my heart being spoken to this moment?" "Where might
this word intersect my own life right now?" And as you ask such
questions, listen. The *meditatio* movement is not a monologue.
It is meant to be a personal conversation with your Beloved.

Lectio divina is a potent way to engage in ongoing, daily dialogue with the Lord. When you listen with the ear of the heart,
Bible reading becomes prayerful conversation. A small heresy
of my Christian upbringing was the idea that Bible reading is
separate or intrinsically different from prayer. I was taught to
study the Bible and then, switching gears, commence praying.
Bible reading is, however, a part of our prayer time and should
not be considered separate.

There are various ways to move through the *meditatio* time.

It can be done internally, noting the interaction of head and heart with God's Word, pondering, allowing those truths and insights to be guests of your deep self. But you may wish to keep a *lectio divina* journal. Here you may record not only your interactions but allow the writing itself to become the ground of interaction. Writing teacher Donald Murray notes that we don't write *what* we know so much as we write *until* we know. I find that using journaling as part of my *meditatio* results in connections that I hadn't realized when I first put my pen to paper. And if you're a visual learner, journaling can be broadened to sketches and drawings of what you're sensing in this movement. We're all individuals, and God relates with each of us uniquely. What matters is to engage in the ways that God is waiting to be found by you.

Don't be concerned about getting some "big message" out of the text. That is a false-self distraction. Even if you don't sense any particular response, stay with the questions—listening, silent. The purpose of *lectio divina* is not to receive a communiqué from God. If nothing seems to come, no matter—something that you are not aware of may be occurring beyond the cognitive level. What's important is to just be with the Lord and his Word.

Through the process of *meditatio,* you will gradually be changed by the Word. Basil Pennington says, "What this *meditatio* does is to change a *notional assent* into a *real assent.* As we receive the words of revelation into our mind, they are just so many notions or ideas, which we accept in faith. We do believe. But as we assimilate them through meditation, our whole being comes to respond to them. We move to a real assent. Our whole being, above all our hearts, says: 'Yes, this is so. This is reality.'"[11]

3. Oratio: The Deep Self Is Touched

Out of your meditation on the passage may emerge a response to God that you want to pray about. Ask yourself, "Out of my interaction with the Word, what do I want to say to God?" Pray about any questions you have in regard to the passage, about any truth God has highlighted for you, and about the will to incorporate that truth into your living. It's important, too, to express gratitude to the Lord for him and his Word. Beyond these good things, *oratio* is a time to not only express your heart's longings but to let God become that longing. Your heart and mind are open to God, and you await him. The prayer is likely to be marked by silences, those spaces of being that are too important to clutter with words.

4. Contemplatio: Rest and Silence

You may want to read through the passage slowly one last time. The point of this reading is not to glean any further insights but to simply soak in, to rest in, the Word. With the seed of the Word sown in your heart, you enter a period of silence and rest before the Lord. Your response to God finds its culmination in *contemplatio:* "Reality becomes so real to us that a word or a movement of the heart can no longer adequately respond to it. Our *whole being* must say 'yes.' This is *contemplatio*."[12] In *contemplatio* you are simply present to God. Here, being completely eclipses doing. God's most intimate language—silence—is your song. You may sit in silence a minute or two—or more if you can—to conclude *lectio divina*. You may also enter more deeply and deliberately into an extended time of silent prayer. The *contemplatio* movement recognizes that there is more to you than imagination and intellect. It recognizes that you do, after all, possess a soul that may rest in God's Word and be spoken to in secret ways if God desires. So, give God room and with your silent openness, allow God to complete the time in any way he likes.

In the practice of *lectio divina*, the schism between the head and heart may be healed, intellect and imagination are welcome, initiation and reception are properly balanced. And in such a discipline, the false self struggles for equilibrium and eventually falters, while the true self takes its place in the banqueting hall of God's love.

The wonder of *lectio divina* is that it transforms not just your private moments with the Lord but the rest of life also. As a result of this practice, the listening heart that awaits the Beloved, awaits him everywhere, sees him everywhere, loves and experiences him everywhere. Macrina Wiederkehr adds, "The incarnational aspect of Christianity reminds us that all of life is full of God. *Lectio Divina,* then, is a way of reading God in everything. . . . The one who is immersed in the Word of God in the Scriptures is eventually able to read God in all things. Divine Reading becomes a way of life."[13]

Centering Prayer: The Heart of Stillness

In Psalm 46 oceans froth, mountains tumble, and the earth itself buckles. In the middle of the din and uproar, comes a familiar verse: "Be still, and know that I am God" (Ps. 46:10). Why should we be still to know God? Isn't his presence and person obvious through his demonstrations of power? But the way to really know God is not through his great strength but through stillness. As it was for Elijah—who understood God was not in the roaring wind, the earthquake, or the fire—often God's most profound arrival is stillness, the gentle whisper that beckons. Stillness is perhaps God's most cherished place to be known by his people.

Although foreign for most of us, there is a place for such tender stillness within our spiritual practices. There is a space we can enter where God's agenda is all, and we simply sit in affectionate silence with our Beloved. If you wish your *lectio divina's contemplatio* movement to be an extended time of quiet contemplation, you will benefit from understanding the practice of centering prayer, which is a prayer of stillness in which you open quietly and intimately to the presence of God.

Centering prayer is an ancient way of silent, restful prayer. Its first recorded practice occurred during the time of the desert fathers and mothers in the early Christian centuries wherein spiritual elders encouraged a type of prayer that used few words. The centering prayer practice reemerged during the 1970s, primarily through the teaching of Thomas Keating and Basil Pennington. Their "repackaging" organized this prayer practice, especially as it is presented in *The Cloud of Unknowing*. The author of *The Cloud* recommends a type of prayer that is nothing but a pure intention of love for God that may gather into a single word, as opposed to the many words that punctuate our prayer times. Centering prayer is a resting in God's presence, beyond thought, image, and emotion. Thoughts, images, and emotions are vital to our active lives with the Lord, but centering prayer presupposes a beneficial place of stillness—a place underneath thought, image, and emotion—where we can just *be* to God.

The centering prayer method contains two spiritual qualities. The first is that this prayer is a prayer of rest, as it is beyond all mental activity. Psalm 23 says God leads us into restful places. "He makes me lie down in green pastures, he leads me beside quiet waters, he restores my soul" (vv. 2–3). Psalm 62:5 encourages. "Find rest, O my soul, in God alone." Scripture connects rest with God's nearness. "He who dwells in the shelter of the Most High will rest in the shadow of the Almighty" (Ps. 91:1). Scripture also associates rest with following God's ways— Stand at the crossroads and look; ask for the ancient paths, ask where the good way is, and walk in it, and you will find rest for your souls" (Jer. 6:16). Rest, then, is a spiritual quality upon which vitality of faith and relationship with God depend.

With the Ten Commandments' concept of Sabbath, God organized rest into an actual day. Sabbath became a way for humanity to imitate God: "Remember the Sabbath day by keeping it holy. Six days you shall labor and do all your work, but the seventh day is a Sabbath to the LORD your God. . . . For in six days the LORD made the heavens and the earth, the sea, and all that is in them, but he rested on the seventh day" (Exod. 20:8–11). The Sabbath also helps us recognize that we are the people of

God: "I gave them my Sabbaths as a sign between us, so they would know that I the LORD made them holy" (Ezek. 20:12). Sabbath is an indispensable, God-designated way to know God and obey him more fully. The writer of Hebrews even connects our entering such rest with resisting the disobedience that characterized the Israelites restless desert wanderings: "There remains, then, a Sabbath-rest for the people of God; for anyone who enters God's rest also rests from his own work, just as God did from his. Let us, therefore, make every effort to enter that rest, so that no one will fall by following their example of disobedience" (Heb. 4:9–11). Just as one day out of seven is set aside to refrain from work and rest in the Lord, so can our spiritual practices contain an element of Sabbath. If Sabbath is part of a way of life, not just a weekly observance, and is pivotal to obeying and believing, then moving toward disciplines that are themselves rest makes sense.

As westerners who struggle with a false self, the heart's posture of rest feels strange, even threatening. We're not good at it, and it seems a dangerous waste of our time to include a discipline of complete rest in our practices. Yet hear Jesus' call to the disciples in Mark 6:31: "Come with me by yourselves to a quiet place and get some rest." Repeat those words to yourself. Does anything stir within you when you hear this invitation? Perhaps a sense of relief, safety, or an at-home feeling? Is it possible that Jesus directs such an invitation to you now? Jesus' words here are the heart of centering prayer—pulling back from noise, distraction, and activity toward a place of restful quiet where we might focus solely on our Lord.

Centering prayer is a prayer of deep rest, but it has a second spiritual quality, that of loving attention to God, of gazing upon his presence, that is rooted in a response to Scripture. Psalm 123 declares, "I lift up my eyes to you, to you whose throne is in heaven. As the eyes of slaves look to the hand of their master, as the eyes of a maid look to the hand of her mistress, so our eyes look to the LORD our God, till he shows us his mercy" (vv. 1–2). This theme of loving attention is central to Psalm 27 where

David says, "One thing I ask of the LORD, this is what I seek: that I may dwell in the house of the LORD all the days of my life, to gaze upon the beauty of the LORD and to seek him in his temple" (v. 4). What does it mean, literally, to watch the hand of the Lord or to gaze upon the beauty of the Lord? These are not just nice ideas or purely poetic utterances; this loving, adoring gaze is the "work" of our rest in centering prayer.

In 2 Corinthians, Paul differentiates between the old covenant and the new by citing the veil that Moses wore to separate the shine of God's glory from the Israelites. In Jesus, no protective veil is needed, and we, like Moses, may encounter God in a more intimate, face-to-face manner: "But we all, with unveiled face, beholding as in a mirror the glory of the Lord, are being transformed into the same image from glory to glory, just as from the Lord, the Spirit" (2 Cor. 3:18 NASB). The New International Version translates "beholding" as "reflect" or "contemplate." This is a beautiful, restful picture of centering prayer: the unveiled face of the true self contemplating the glory of God. Attentively dwelling in the presence of God is our most potent and supreme source of transformation. We can only be transformed into God's image by focusing our gaze, our attention, to the glory of that image. We must ask whether this contemplation, this gazing upon the Lord, is to be taken seriously in our disciplines or whether it's, again, just a poetic way of speaking. This gazing brings us not only into an awareness of God's presence, which in itself is wonderful, but opens all that we are to that presence. We find ourselves, lovingly, literally, in the presence of God. And where else should we be when our disciplines find their culmination?

You may well wonder if centering prayer is a type of Eastern or New Age meditation. It is not. These meditations have to do with emptying the mind, detachment without an infilling of God, and being caught up in some sort of universal spirit or Nirvana. Centering prayer is contemplative, meaning it was created to contemplate, to focus on the true God. It is unfortunate that in many faith circles any desire to enter into quietness in prayer, to come toward resting in the Presence, to set aside our busy, materialistic intellect, is automatically identified as evil or unbiblical. Pennington helps to further distinguish contemplative prayer practice from Eastern meditation: "The typical Eastern technique, seeking to achieve something in itself by the very activity of the one performing it, demands absolute fidelity to the technique until the end is attained. For the Christian, prayer is always a response. God initiates the activity, and indeed is the source of our response."[14]

In centering prayer we pass through more active ways of engaging with the Lord, ways that, profitable as they are, are mediated by thought, image, or emotion. Centering prayer seeks an unmediated coming into Presence, where we sit in stillness, holding deep within our childlike intention to be absorbed in the Lord's beauty and holiness.

The method of centering prayer is simple, which is part of the prayer's attraction. You need not be caught up in complex techniques, but some important points for how to enter centering prayer may prove helpful.[15]

1. Preparing for the Prayer

Find a quiet place that's as free as possible from distractions and noises in which to do your *lectio divina* and centering prayer. Centering prayer is a time of extended contemplation that follows *lectio divina,* because such a quiet, loving gaze is a natural outgrowth of receiving the Word of God. Get comfortable. Those who practice centering prayer recommend sitting in a relaxed position, preferably with back support, but not one that will encourage you to nod off. Close your eyes for the prayer time since so much of our mental energy surrounds sight. Often I'll begin my centering prayer time with words, such as "May I rest in your Presence" or "May I bask in your beauty." The ancients suggest starting the prayer time with "O God, come to my assistance; O Lord, make haste to help me."

2. The Challenge of Thoughts

In centering prayer, the desire is to sit undivided in the presence of the Lord. One problem with entering into such quiet is that thoughts will inevitably tug for attention upon your awareness. Some of these thoughts might be your to-do list for the day, concerns and conflicts you need to work out, or even your own self-reflection on the prayer time. Interacting with your thoughts divides your attention from God. It's like sitting in the most beautiful cathedral ever built but only noticing the fly that's buzzing near you. This metaphor, unfortunately, characterizes too much of our disciplines and our day. Centering prayer seeks to focus upon the Lord with all that we are and to put aside the tyranny of thoughts, which constantly bid for our attention.

Let me be clear: centering prayer is *not* about making the mind a blank (as in Eastern meditation). Rather, it seeks to direct our full attention to the Lord. Paul declares in 2 Corinthians, "We take captive every thought to make it obedient to Christ" (10:5). Thoughts and images are welcome to flit about our minds, but—and this is the key—we need not *think* about these images and thoughts. Thomas Keating says that centering prayer is not about what's in your mind but about your detachment from what's in your mind. We seek to abstain not so much from thoughts as from our commentary about these thoughts. These running commentaries spark interior dialogue that is characterized by emotions and reactions, which are the guts of the false self. It is from these commentaries, dialogues, and subsequent emotions that we rest during the prayer.[16] Returning to the metaphor above, you can sit in your beautiful cathedral, enthralled with the gilded ceiling, admiring the graceful arches and stained glass while vaguely aware that the fly is buzzing nearby. You can even notice it darting about in your peripheral vision, but you choose to keep your eyes on the majestic, abstaining from the internal commentary about the fly's annoying presence. Pennington has this to add: "Much of the time, while we set our hearts upon the Lord, our mind and imagination amuse themselves and fill the time with their own devices. Little matter. We need not concern ourselves about it. Our heart is set upon the Lord. We are in deep prayer, in heart-to-heart communion with our Lord. . . . We pray in response to God's great love, to give our hearts to him. The rest is inconsequential."[17]

3. The Prayer Word: An Expression of Intention

Inevitably, though, some small insect of thought dives into my attention and pulls me out of my conscious abiding in God's presence. When this occurs—and it does—how can I return to my loving gaze as quickly and as effortlessly as possible? To help reexpress my intention to simply be with God, I choose a prayer word before the prayer starts.

Whenever thoughts go from floating in the wings to commentating on center stage, the prayer word asserts what my true intention is, which is to gaze upon the Lord and to consent to his work within me. This word is generally a name associated with God (God, Jesus, Father, Abba, Yahweh, El Shaddai) or some special quality about God (love, peace, trust, mercy, grace). The prayer word helps me to quickly realign myself to God's presence when my thinking divides my attention. Unlike a mantra, which is repeated for its own sake, the word is used gently anytime during the prayer when thoughts become intrusive. Sometimes I use the prayer word often; other times not at all. The word has no power, in any event, and its sole purpose is to express in one simple word my desire to be absorbed in God's presence. It is, ultimately, a small token of love for my Beloved to whom I open.

The time of centering prayer is traditionally concluded with silently repeating the Lord's Prayer or praying a selected psalm. This mental prayer is helpful for the transition from your place of deep rest to the flow of activity that will follow. Practitioners recommend that centering prayer be done for twenty minutes, once or twice a day. If you like, you can set a timer (as long as it has a gentle alarm) so that you won't be tempted to think about the prayer's length. Even if you start out with five minutes dedicated to this prayer, it's still a worthwhile discipline. Centering prayer is not meant to replace other ways of praying. Instead, it complements the ways in which we already pray, recognizing, as evidenced in Scripture, that God calls us to different ways of praying at different times (such as prayers of adoration, thanksgiving, intercession, and so on).

Our motives for entering this practice—and for the disciplines generally—must be purified of the competitive framework. Because this prayer is beyond thoughts, images, and emotion, its value cannot be judged by what you experience during the prayer. And what you experience, especially at first, may be resistance and struggle. Setting aside your busy thoughts feels difficult and unnatural at first, and your centering prayer time might be one huge tussle with your thoughts. The calming of your psyche can be conditioned through repetition, and God is your help. Others are so unaccustomed to stillness except at day's end that they will automatically become drowsy. It doesn't matter whether you find yourself distracted, drifting off into slumber, or suddenly caught up in the heavenlies. Avoid measuring or judging how you perform this or any other discipline. Your intent is everything. You come only to be with God, to intentionally abide in him who is your life, and the presence or absence of distractions, feelings, and such can't affect the prayer's worth or how much God treasures it.

The fruit of centering prayer—and the benchmark to discern whether or not this prayer is really for you—comes outside the time of the prayer. The prayer may or may not be accentuated with a sense of peace and quiet love—oftentimes it is. But such things must not determine any future fidelity to this prayer. As with all the disciplines, their worth comes in whether the time lived around them is characterized by a deeper love for God, as expressed in the fruit of the Spirit (Gal. 5:22–23). In as much as godly, love-filled fruit grows out of your living, this prayer is likely a helpful discipline.

In the Arms of Abba

Centering prayer sounds like a practice aimed at believers who enjoy silence, who crave quiet, and who lead slow enough lives to make this prayer "work." But centering prayer is not dependent upon temperament or personality. It is a discipline open to all as the Lord leads. David Johnson is the preaching pastor at Church of the Open Door in Maple Grove, Minnesota, an evangelical church known for its strong Bible teaching. Raised as the son of a Baptist minister, David attended a Christian college and conservative seminaries. He also regularly engages in centering prayer and, in light of his own driven personality, considers himself an unlikely candidate for such a practice.

David entered into centering prayer during a time of great fatigue marked by the struggle to stay fully engaged with the busyness of ministry and life. After attending a conference that stressed renewed energy and vigor in ministry, David realized he needed centering prayer: "I knew if I was going to keep up, I had to slow down. For me, in order to keep up the pace, I needed to learn how to be quiet in the presence of God, how to listen, particularly because I'm a type 'A' person. In order for me to do what I do, to be who I am, I need this discipline." He views centering prayer as indispensable for enlarging his sense of God's holiness and for "passionately pursuing God and knowing him in every way possible." While not all people may feel drawn to centering prayer specifically, silence and solitude before the Lord are essential for authentic discipleship.

And at the core of this discipleship is the emergence of the true self that unfolds as we reside in the presence of God. One great value of centering prayer is that no other spiritual discipline so thoroughly confronts and disrupts the false-self system. The false self has nothing to hold onto—no measurement, no progress, no product. There is only our presence with Presence. Centering prayer, by its very nature, calls out the one self that can abide in God's presence: the true self.

Centering prayer, then, is our consent, our "yes," to be whom God created us to be. Pennington comments, "This is the first step of the Centering Prayer method: going beyond the false self and all that constructs it. . . . Once we are there, we are prayer. By accepting to be who we are, we pray. There is nothing more. And there could be nothing more. For we have entered into the fullness of God."[18] Here, prayer is a state of being—our whole and actual self, our very essence, becomes prayer to God.

The motive for centering prayer is simple devotion for God alone. So your motivation for this discipline is purer, and that purity is love itself. Using father-child imagery, Pennington describes the intimate, innocent bond of love that is the heart of centering prayer: "A father is delighted when his little one, leaving off his toys and his friends, runs to him and climbs in his arms. As he holds his little one close to him, he cares little whether his child is looking around, his attention flitting from one thing to another, or if he is intent upon his father, or just settling down to sleep. Essentially the child is choosing to be with his father, confident of the love, the care, the security in those arms. Our centering prayer is much like that."[19] Does Pennington's assessment and imagery of centering prayer—you, the child, comforted in the arms of Abba—seem too incredible, too fantastic? Consider Psalm 131, which reflects the intimacy of David's prayer relationship with God:

> My heart is not proud, O LORD,
>   my eyes are not haughty;
> I do not concern myself with great matters
>   or things too wonderful for me.
> But I have stilled and quieted my soul;
>   like a weaned child with its mother,
>   like a weaned child is my soul within me.
> O Israel, put your hope in the LORD
>   both now and forevermore.

This prayer experience mirrors centering prayer, describing an intimate joining, a silent communing, where prayer is a state of being. Realizing the smallness of his own mind, David turns away from thoughts and perceptions, experiencing the wonder of stillness in God. Remarkably, David, the great warrior of Israel, describes himself as sitting like "a weaned child with its mother." A weaned child no longer needs mother's milk, so snuggling with the mother, who is obviously God, is not about expectation. The child longs to be taken up into the mother's arms just for the comfort, the loving union with the parent. This portrait of childlike affection and vulnerability is difficult for most of us to imagine experiencing with God.

Some of us are attracted to such a union yet lament a lack of time for these practices. While there are legitimate time constraints, we must discern whether or not our busyness is driven by the false self. Perhaps you are saying, "These practices won't work for me. My image of God is too distorted. My movements toward Christ too limited by mistrust." That's precisely *why* you need disciplines such as *lectio divina* and centering prayer. They can mark for you the beginning of wholeness. Entering into such disciplines, the schism between head and heart begins to heal, and the Word of the Lord is accomplished: "They will be my people, and I will be their God. I will give them singleness of heart and action" (Jer. 32:38–39). The false self becomes swallowed up in dialogue with, and loving attention to, our precious Lord.

Centering prayer is our love gift to God, the only gift our Beloved desires: our whole self. From this still, loving gaze flows the things that, in our self-made discipleship, we strive to "achieve": obedience, holiness, worship. This is the emergence of the true self, the person we've waited our whole lives to find. The spiritual life we've searched for, the spiritual self for whom we've hoped, is now realized within our disciplines because we have at last recognized ourselves in the embrace of Christ, our heart's true home.

Coming Home

Contemplative practices, ancient as they are, can become new in your daily life with the Lord. I can convey to you technique and method, but the thread that weaves through the entire discussion is love. There's no point to contemplation—or to *any* spiritual discipline—if you're not lead into deeper awareness of, and receptivity to, the love of God. By its very nature, contemplation is receiving God's love and calling out your true self. Thelma Hall says contemplative prayer "is an effect of being literally 'in love' with God, at the deepest level of the relationship with him for which we are created."[20] If all of your disciplines, contemplative or not, do not tenderly lead you into falling more in love with Jesus Christ, then they are corrupted, impotent, bankrupt.

Lectio divina and centering prayer are about finding ourselves immersed in love, safe in the lap of our Beloved, which is to say they're about coming home. These and other disciplines can lead us to bask in the beauty of the Lord and to hear his declaration: "I have loved you with an everlasting love; I have drawn you with loving-kindness" (Jer. 31:3).

Perhaps you're not used to receiving the love of Jesus in any of your spiritual practices. If you do not find the lavish love of God in your spiritual disciplines, then you will look elsewhere, and your exile from the Father's house will continue to haunt your journey. Henri Nouwen says, "I am the prodigal son every time I search for unconditional love where it cannot be found. Why do I keep ignoring the place of true love and persist in looking for it elsewhere?"[21] Our images of the disciplines as the marriage bed, as a place of rest for our hearts, are either absent or so arid that our thirst drives us to lesser places. But we were made for one love, created for one God. And all we really want, in our heart of hearts, is to find our way home.

We walk our asphalt realities, fellowship with others, and try to live a God-honoring life, but if we're honest and aware, we recognize an ache, a hunger that is not satiated. We realize our strong desire is to be cherished for our being, not our doing, to be forever united with the only One who will ever truly know and understand us. We were built to long for heaven now, and our contemplative practices give us a wondrous taste—a glimpse—of heaven. Jesus' words, "Now this is eternal life: that they may know you, the only true God . . ." (John 17:3), beautifully merge with "Be still, and know . . . " (Ps. 46:10).

And in receiving the love of God, your life will find its complete and perfect work, which is loving God back in the manner that you yourself are loved. The heart of contemplative practices is enthrallment with Presence, the underlying desire to abide with the very person of God. And nothing else is sought beyond this—no deeper thought, emotion, or experience. Here, we love God not for his works, for his blessings, or for the other external clues of his Presence but for himself: "In the contemplative work God is loved above every creature purely and simply for his own sake. Indeed, the very heart of this work is nothing else but a naked intent toward God for his own sake."[22] This "naked intent" comprises the substance of contemplation, creating the foundation of our spiritual practices and of life itself.

And loving God back is not merely a part of our disciplines, something we take an hour or two here and there to send heavenward. This love is about living a certain kind of life, a life where even to breathe is to worship. The anonymous author of *The Cloud of Unknowing,* penning his thoughts in obscurity seven hundred years ago, provides a powerful summation on the simple love that is our naked intent: "For I tell you this, one loving blind desire for God alone is more valuable in itself, more pleasing to God and to the saints, more beneficial to your own growth, and more helpful to your friends . . . than anything else you could do."[23]

8

LIVING THE
INTENTIONAL LIFE

Earth's crammed with heaven,
And every common bush afire with God;
But only he who sees takes off his shoes;
The rest sit round it and pluck blackberries.
                    —Elizabeth Barrett Browning

As we go on into God we shall see the excellency of the life of
constant communion where all thoughts and acts are prayer, and
the entire life becomes one holy sacrifice of praise and worship.
                    —A. W. Tozer

And this is the testimony: God has given us eternal life, and this
life is in his Son. He who has the Son has life; he who does not
have the Son of God does not have life.
                    —John the Apostle (1 John 5:11–12)

Almost every church has them. People who exude joy, who are peaceful, settled, whose very presence issues an indictment against a lackluster version of Christian living. They talk about life as if Jesus is actually with them in the office and in the grocery store, peering at them over the laundry basket. Such people exhibit Christ in genuine ways. You can't help but be attracted to them—as well as haunted by them. Earlier in my Christian life, I wondered what their secret was, how they managed to get more of Jesus than the rest of us. I did my spiritual disciplines, engaged in godly service, tried to connect the dots spiritually, yet something was missing. I experienced a blockage of that love and trust and fullness in my daily living. Do you ever feel there's a spiritual glass ceiling? That other people live with an abundance of joy, meaning, and purpose—but not you? Do you bump against this transparent barrier, devouring devotionals or attending prayer conferences, with your days largely remaining the same?

Even if the windows of heaven are flung open during your spiritual practices, what happens to the hours afterward? The disciplines are meant to add Christ's love and tender abiding to our lives. But often this kind of fullness dangles just beyond the glass, eluding us. Our spiritual practices, even contemplative ones, are only as powerful as the life lived around them. But the message we're sometimes given by Christian culture is to do the spiritual disciplines, rendering to God his due while rendering to Caesar the rest of the day.

A popular phrase asks, "What would Jesus do?" The question suggests that the Christian life is simply a matter of pausing, thinking a dilemma through, and then deciding on the proper course of behavior. For those on the cusp of new life in Christ, asking "What would Jesus do?" might be instructive. But as we deepen into Christ, we realize that Christian living does not consist of answers to exam questions or of spiritualized behavior modification. In this approach to faith, Christ-in-me is really more like Christ-around-the-corner-from-me.

This approach, too, creates a serious disconnection between spiritual disciplines and the rest of life. And the dilemma of the spiritual glass ceiling is that the tender moments in our practices and the breakthrough moments in Sunday worship or on the spiritual retreat cannot be replicated in our daily living. The Israelites took the separation of disciplines and life to new heights, and in Isaiah 58, God confronts their sin. Through the great prophet, God speaks:

> "Why have we fasted," they say, "and you have not seen it? Why have we humbled ourselves, and you have not noticed?" Yet on the day of your fasting, you do as you please and exploit all your workers. Your fasting ends in quarreling and strife, and in striking each other with wicked fists. You cannot fast as you do today and expect your voice to be heard on high. Is this the kind of fast I have chosen, only a day for a man to humble himself? Is it only for bowing one's head like a reed and for lying on sackcloth and ashes? Is that what you call a fast, a day acceptable to the LORD? (vv. 3–5)

God's critique of the Israelites had nothing to do with the regularity or the technique of their fasting. The accusation was that their fasting did not complete itself in righteous actions. The Israelites divorced acts of devotion to God from how they actually lived. Certainly such a response was partly born of callused hearts, but it also points to the problem of compartmentalizing, of separating the disciplines from the rest of life. We, like they, tend to isolate spiritual practices as one slice of life and our activities as another much larger piece of the pie. If we separate the two, we come to see the disciplines as privatized experiences and as an end in themselves.

When disciplines are divorced from the rest of living, finding Christ's presence in daily life becomes optional or extra. For the majority of my life, I thought of my activities—my working, my initiating, my doing—as a series of events to recover from: I go out, get depleted, return home. Once there, I lock the door and refresh myself in the private place with God. Dallas Willard comments, "We've somehow encouraged a separation of our faith from everyday life. We've relegated God's life in us to special times and places and states of mind. . . . When we think of 'taking Christ into the workplace' or 'keeping Christ in the home,' we are making our faith into a set of *special* acts. The 'specialness' of such acts just underscores the point—that being a Christian, being Christ's, isn't thought of as a normal part of life."[1]

If this is your perception, then the disciplines are only a private refuge, a rejuvenating sanctuary, your personal spa. But God inextricably links the disciplines with living when he says, "Is not this the kind of fasting I have chosen: to loosen the chains of injustice and untie the cords of the yoke, to set the oppressed free?" (Isa. 58:6). Compassion toward others is not only the proper end of the disciplines, but God promises that in compassionate living, "You will be like a well-watered garden, like a spring whose waters never fail" (v. 11).

I had everything turned around. I believed that when I returned, battle weary, and engaged with God in the disciplines, then I was the "well-watered garden," then I became the "spring whose waters never fail," then and only then did I truly feel refreshed and satisfied. But that's not what this Scripture is saying. Our call to be the verdant garden, the refreshing spring, comes not just in the midst of our private spiritual practices but in all the noise and stress of daily work.

When did we settle on the idea that life is more or less a string of tiring events to endure? When did we decide that the fullness of God is in a secret place, and Presence is muted in the marketplace? Our community of faith, with our assumptions and closed-off hearts, has turned the potentially well-watered garden into a desert. And there's nothing we can "do" about it. Rather, we must come to see life differently through a revolutionary awareness of reality as it really is. And from such a place, consent to live an intentional life.

The Danger of Spiritual Apartheid

What do I mean by an intentional life? It means living from a strong, God-filled inner sanctuary, rather than skimming the surface of life, hydroplaning in a series of reactions to the environment. Living the intentional life entails our understanding that we are called to a countercultural way of life, different even from what faith communities might model. Ephesians 5 gives a picture of intentional living: "For you were once darkness, but now you are light in the Lord. Live as children of light. . . . This is why it is said: 'Wake up, O sleeper, rise from the dead, and Christ will shine on you.' Be very careful, then, how you live—not as unwise but as wise, making the most of every opportunity, because the days are evil. . . . Speak to one another with psalms, hymns and spiritual songs. Sing and make music in your heart to the Lord, always giving thanks to God the Father for everything, in the name of our Lord Jesus Christ" (vv. 8, 14–16, 19–20). Like the misguided believers Paul is trying to rouse, we, too, rarely move in the fullness of our spiritual inheritance. We are called to much more. The trouble is, most of us drowse through our daily lives as if separated from Christ. We've forgotten how to live our lives as a thankful song.

How might you awaken to see life differently? First, you must confront how spiritual apartheid has plundered your awareness of God.

I like to talk about spiritual apartheid during a morning class, say 8 A.M. About twenty students slouch before me, barely awake, ready for another morning of mundane composition instruction on the five rules for comma usage or something equally exciting. But the concept applies to any situation that has become routine, expected, and lifeless: the morning breakfast table, the cubicle at work, or the tedious line at the grocery store. So, I face these students, most of whom genuinely desire God in their lives, and my little speech to them goes something like this: "If you are sitting in my class right now and your awareness of, and receptivity to, God is any less than when you are sitting in church attentively worshiping on a Sunday morning, then you are a victim of spiritual apartheid. This means you have decided God cannot be found in this time and place, and you have turned yourself off to anything he might want to

say to you or to show you during this hour that we're together."
This gets their attention, but it's so foreign to them, they have
little idea what to do with it. But understanding spiritual apart-
held and how it tears our consciousness away from God is essential if we desire to live an intentional life.

The term, *spiritual apartheid*, coined by William Shannon, is
"the mentality that sets God apart from creation."[2] *Apartheid*
refers to South Africa's former policy of racial separation; spiritual apartheid is the belief that God is more present and active
in certain times and places than in others. We shut God out of
our consciousness during those moments that we label as
nonspiritual, which constitute the majority of our day. Of course,
such decisions are unspoken, but a fluctuating awareness of
God, tuning in and out depending upon the setting, keeps us
in the grip of spiritual apartheid. And within spiritual apartheid is a profound error about the nature of kingdom reality
and a profound arrogance as well.

Our allegiance to spiritual apartheid is expressed in numerous ways. Have you ever signed up for a church retreat, saying,
"I really need to get away from it all and be with God"? Or you
might decide on a missions trip, thinking, "I need to be in a
place where I can see God truly at work." Or you may visit the
church across town because "the Spirit really moves there." The
assumption is that God's presence is incomplete or diluted where
you are and fails to press through the routine of your life. Thus,
to be filled with the presence of God, you must go elsewhere
because your daily duties are marked by absence.

Such "getaway" experiences are sometimes held up as a cure-
all for our unawareness of God's presence because they appear
to work. We might return from the retreat fired up and refreshed. We begin to believe some activities have a certain power
or godly panache to them. And we are lulled into the heresy
that God is more available to us in those places.[3] But what is
truly different from those experiences as opposed to our regular lives? God and his presence are certainly the same. The
difference is our openness to his presence and our willingness

to walk in awareness of God. We expect to meet God at the retreat, to hear him speak, and to receive something of spiritual value from him. And then after two days on the mount, we come home, and the mundane begins all over again; the legitimate spiritual good God poured into us eventually dims. And when we again thirst for the presence of the Lord, we sign up for another retreat to quench our longing.

To live in spiritual apartheid is to be constantly making judgments about the spirituality of the different times and places we encounter. God shows up here but not as much there. And our judgments demonstrate themselves every time we block God's voice and divide his presence from the present moment.

Perhaps our daily routines are not a God-absent wasteland from which we need to recover and repair. And, maybe, the answer to our lethargy is not more retreats, missions trips, church ministry, and the like. What we need, to use Paul's words, is to wake up, to consent to no longer be dead to God for the bulk of our days.

The hours are already God-drenched. They couldn't be more so. But spiritual apartheid devastates our awareness of God, and we move about our day, wherein Christ is little more than a rumor. We cannot live an intentional life unless we confront the ways that spiritual apartheid darkens our spiritual selves. If God becomes more and more the center of our awareness, not just in church or on the retreat but in the fast-food line, in evening rush hour, in the walk to the company conference room, we will begin to live fully and intentionally.

Living in the Present Moment

I was in the second year of my teaching career. To make ends meet, I taught half-time at two schools. Splitting time between two campuses is a horrendous way to make a living, and nearly every class was a new preparation. I have never been as harried, busy, and mentally fatigued as I was during that year. When my poetry literature class ended at 11:30, I had twenty-five minutes to drive to the other campus, park, and begin my freshman composition class. Afterward, I rushed back to the first campus to teach again. My lunchtime consisted of eating whatever portable food I could munch while in transit.

One day when my literature class had just ended, I grabbed an apple out of my bag and walked out to my car. Suddenly something broke through my preoccupation with the class I had just taught and my concern about finding a parking space at the next campus. I was in the moment. The apple in my hand, a Granny Smith, so firm and tart, drew my attention. It was delicious. And as I reveled in the apple, I was dazzled by the miracle of gold and red leaves in the crisp, late September air. It was as if a window had been opened. For a few seconds, where I was and what surrounded me was more important than where I had been or where I was going. Even years later, I cherish that moment of consolation during a difficult and uncertain year.

If we wish to be delivered from spiritual apartheid, we must first consent to live in the moment, a place that, paradoxically, we're always in but rarely enter. Rootedness in the present moment is to live in simple awareness. As with my apple story, simple awareness is to be present to your surroundings within the moment. It is to notice things, to engage with all the colors, events, and people and, thus, to drink deeply from the cup of your own life. Simple awareness isn't profound, but it is rare. You might protest, "Don't we all live in the present?" Bodily, yes. But in our conscious selves, we routinely refuse the present moment.

If we reject the present moment, where are we to go? There are two primary destinations: the past and the future. Movements into the past are motivated by regret and revision while pushing into the future is about control.

Pat was an off-and-on member of a support group I was once a part of, and one of her return visits was instructive for me. As usual, her sharing was a small tirade, detailing how her husband had left her for another woman, how her life has been a wreck since that time, and how she told him off or wished she had. The separation and divorce occurred years ago, but for Pat, the papers had been signed yesterday. Her anguish and fury were that fresh. In the middle of her tearful story, an incredibly sad thought came to me: "Pat's whole life is designed to accommodate the care and feeding of her wounded memories." Pat never lived in the present moment, instead she lead a life of regret.

Do you replay hurtful experiences in your head? Many of us bathe ourselves in regret over our wounds, not so as to heal but as an activity in and of itself. The essential energy of Pat's life was regret over her perceived misfortunes, and she never moved on. Many among us are similarly hooked by the past, never realizing that regret is a universe without God. Regret asserts that something is forever beyond the healing and restoration of our sovereign Lord.

Along with fueling regret, we also lodge ourselves in the past in order to revise it. As a rather shy person who innately dislikes confrontation, I sometimes don't say everything I need to say when I'm hurt or confused. So I squander time in the present, internally creating long speeches, what I wished I'd said to my colleague, my friend, or the checkout clerk. I visualize different endings to conflicts wherein I triumph. When we do such things, we're trying to revise something that has already been settled in terms of time and space. As delusional as this is, revisional living tends to assuage the false self.

As frequent as living in the past can be, forays into the future are just as common and destructive. The competitive framework is strongly exercised here, where the present moment is simply the rest stop on the road to some future destination. Life is treated as a dress rehearsal, and we say, "This is all preparation for something else, something better because someday, my life will really begin and then . . ." (fill in the blank with some wonderful, ego-satisfying event). We always seem to be living in wait for something else. We are tantalized by phrases such as when I grow up . . . when I finish school . . . when I get

my dream job . . . when I get married . . . when I have kids . . .
when my vacation comes . . . when the kids are out of the
house . . . when I retire. The dazzle of destination becomes
greater than what lies within the moment. So we excuse ourselves from being present *now*, abstain from living *now*.

Examining the future with its options and directions is not a
bad thing—not to do so would be unwise. The problem is both
the degree to which the present is forsaken and the level of
fear about what lurks in the future. I see it on my students'
clueless and panicked faces when they recount how the relatives ask, "So, what are your plans after graduation?" I see it,
too, in the expressions of friends who, in midlife, find their
professional life collapsing like a cheap card table or who endure changes in marriages and families. They see the future as
a fearful thing to be managed.

Obsession with the future reflects the drive for control, a
primary hallmark of the false self. We are afraid that our future will not adequately satisfy our old-self needs for security,
esteem, and power, so we manipulate our future moments at
the expense of our present ones. The underlying belief here is
that God isn't entirely trustworthy. It's the serpent's lie carried
over from the Garden: God may not truly have your best inter-
ests in mind. Maybe he isn't entirely good, so take matters into
your own hands.

The Latin phrase *age quod agis* means "do what you are doing."[4] Whatever your activity, give your whole attention, your
whole self, to it for its own sake without calculating what comes
next. Don't go to work in the morning so that you can get
together with friends in the evening. Don't fold your clean laundry so that you can take a walk afterward. Don't attend your
classes simply to have the right information for the test. Be
completely present to your tasks. Our competitive consciousness makes everything we do a stepping-stone to something
else. One moment is just the means to the next, and we move
mindlessly through our days. And as we exist in this way, we
never arrive. We push and push, lunging toward whatever

sparkles ahead, only to find that we spent our days refusing to live. Jesus promised abundance, but abundance is only possible within awareness of the present moment.

Almost everyone can identify with some of these spiritually dangerous excursions away from the present moment. As true-self-emerging believers, we must repent of the regret and revision that pull us into the past and of the drive for control that propels us into the future. To consent to live grounded in the present moment, according to one writer, is a broadening of our obedience to the tenth commandment, "You shall not covet." To covet is to "desire that which is not mine and which I cannot lawfully acquire."[5] Forsaking the present moment is attempting to own events from the past or to acquire from the future that which is solely under God's ownership.

Living in the present moment requires radical trust in God and is one of the greatest compliments we can ever pay to Christ. Covenanting to abide within the present moment is an act of faith because it expresses belief in God's sovereignty beyond Sunday sermons. A life dedicated to the present moment requires trust, and trust requires abandonment, as Jeanne Guyon clarifies: "What is abandonment? It is forgetting your past; it is leaving the future in His hands; it is devoting the present fully and completely to your Lord. Abandonment is being satisfied with the present moment, no matter what it contains. You are satisfied because you know that whatever the moment has, it contains—in that instant—God's eternal plan for you."[6] Such abandonment is difficult, but present-moment trust brings us to truth we must stake our lives upon: that God is good and that everything we most need is available to us now.

Stewardship of the moment begins with coming present to reality and to your own heart. Notice, pay attention. You are continually surrounded with brilliant wonders as well as dark desolation. Whether your inner and outer life is a garden or a desert, say "yes" to all of it. Too much of life is spent fortressing ourselves against the heaviness of life and admitting only happiness or joy. But we can't say, "I'll be present to glad things and ignore that which is unpleasant." That's not how life works. It's all or nothing. We're either present to our lives or we're not.

Practicing the Presence of God

Has a moment ever opened before you like a rose, petal by petal, and you suddenly saw, suddenly understood, that you were there with God, fully alive, and it was enough? Such times are rare, and many wonder why opening to God's presence is so difficult. Without abiding in the present moment, it is nearly impossible. But when we are willing to live attentively in the dailyness of apples and laundry, we will find God as the treasure buried in the field of the present. The God of forever is Lord of the moment. Thus, present-moment awareness opens us to eternity. Rootedness in the present holds within it the possibility of this deeper, more eternal awareness.[7]

Awareness of God must not be confused with simply possessing thoughts about God. Thoughts about God are, of course, valuable, but our post-Enlightenment Christian culture tells us a steady stream of thoughts about God is the highest form of awareness of God. But such thoughts can actually divide us from Presence. Analyzing God tends to make him into an object, something we take out and examine. William Shannon says, "As soon as we try to grasp God in our thought and reflection (that is, as soon as we make God the Object of our thoughts and reflection) God disappears from our consciousness. What replaces our consciousness of God's Presence is the construct of our thoughts and words: not God, but what we think or say about God."[8]

Deep awareness of God, however, is a state of being within the moment, not an activity we undertake, although it can exist within activity. While it may begin with thoughts about God, awareness is something other than this: "A true sense of awareness reduces the distance between me and what I am aware of. A very deep sense of attentive awareness closes the gap between me and that of which I am aware. It brings us together. It unites."[9] We're so used to having our thoughts form the basis of our relationship with God, we scarcely know what spiritual relating is apart from them. What is this deeper, more uniting, type of awareness?

This awareness is the *practice of the presence of God,* a term that comes from a small book by that title. It is the highest degree of awareness and the most excellent fulfillment of living in the present moment. A seventeenth-century monk, Brother Lawrence, had a series of conversations that were written down by an interviewer and published. Brother Lawrence had an amazing capacity to continuously set himself in God's presence. He was the dishwasher in the monastery, and his sense of God's presence was as strong amid the clang and clatter of the busy kitchen as when he was on his knees in his prayer cell. His interviewer says, "With him the set times of prayer were not different from other times. . . . He retired to pray, according to the directions of his superior, but . . . he did not want such retirement, nor ask for it, because his greatest business did not divert him from God."[10] For Brother Lawrence, whether working or in a posture of prayer, there was no qualitative difference in his awareness of God or his receptivity to the Spirit.

Practicing God's presence is another way of following Paul's command to "pray continually" (1 Thess. 5:17). For most of my life I'd considered prayer as worded thought directed to God either silently or aloud. How limiting. Prayer, as discussed in the last chapter, can also be embodied in *who* I am and *how* I am. And, indeed, continual praying is not an activity done in a vacuum; in a sense, I pray at every point in my day.

Leanne Payne points out that if we do not practice the presence of God, we will practice the presence of another—parents, friends, spouse, boss—attuning our deep selves to someone or something. The performing and degraded selves attune to damaging lies that were internalized in childhood. God's presence is not being practiced anytime self-hatred is present. Living in the Lord's presence is, in fact, key to healing those trapped in the false self. The true self emerges when God's love-filled presence is our single prayer and focus.

What does it mean to practice the presence of God? How do you do it? Practicing God's presence is not a feeling, a sensible experience of God, or specific thoughts about God—although any of these may accompany this practice, encourage it, and surround it. Begin by recollecting the reality of God's loving nearness, his attraction to you. Dwell on such truths as you operate throughout your day. Small, wordless prayers begin to occur within you as naturally as breathing. Two prime markers of dwelling in God's presence—compassion and gratitude—arise more and more as God's love becomes your only reality. You choose to receive Jesus as your fond companion, your best self, as you live in the present moment. And as you say with confidence, "Another lives in me," a deep mutual abiding begins— you in Christ, Christ in you.

Practicing the Presence, then, is a continuous receiving and giving of the love of God, an opening to the mystery of God as you live in his presence. It is a receptive posture of unhindered listening and loving. Brother Lawrence believed that "our only business was to love and delight ourselves in God," and "his prayer was nothing else but a sense of the presence of God, his soul being at that time insensible to everything but divine love."[11] Practicing the Presence is assent to living in God's presence and assent to the love that is his presence. It's a response to Jesus' invitation, "Now remain in my love" (John 15:9).

Practicing the Presence is not an activity but an alignment of life, a posture, and, thus, a way of seeing. Through practicing the Presence, you awaken to incarnational reality, where you begin to see God everywhere—all is awash in the wonder of the world that he has made. You become living proof that God dwells in the world and makes his home within as your true self, Christ-in-me: "Christ descends to us and into us. He incarnates us. We are indwelt, in-godded."[12] The glory of God is here and now, as Jesus reminds us: "The kingdom of God is within you" (Luke 17:21). But with spiritual apartheid at work, we tend not to live in this manner, routinely giving mental assent but remaining unmoved. To fully embrace incarnational reality requires both head and heart to be of one accord. It is not sufficient to merely "think" that "the kingdom of God within me" is true; to fully open the will, to wake up, requires the "yes" of both head and heart so that incarnational reality saturates all that you think, do, and are.

Let's say that you're in love—deeply, madly, head over heels—a love that buoys you and electrifies with infatuation and excitement. Even when you're not speaking directly with your beloved, you carry him or her with you, and that love colors everything in a way that is not mere emotion. You are, in essence, abiding in the other. Now, imagine that you are abiding not in the love of a mere human but in Christ, and there is no absence from the force of that love. You carry him everywhere at all times, and this all-powerful love utterly transforms you. We know that we *are* the beloved, and all is changed. The morning car pool, the supermarket produce section, the neighborhood stroll—nothing is again seen or experienced the same. Such is the case for those in Christ; his love burns deep, and we not only see that fire, we are transformed into fire. It is, to use Thomas Kelly's word, to live a God-enthralled life. And everything we do is aflame with love. Here, thought and action, prayer and activity become one because all is for the love of Christ. In speaking of Brother Lawrence, his interviewer says, "He had always been governed by love, without selfish views; and that having resolved to make the love of God the end of all his actions, he had found reasons to be well satisfied with his method. That he was pleased when he could take up a straw from the ground for the love of God, seeking Him only, and nothing else, not even His gifts."[13] As we practice the Presence, everything we do becomes an act of devotion. If life's intent becomes to "Love the Lord your God . . . with all your strength" (Mark 12:30), then each action takes on new significance. Brushing our teeth, washing dishes, driving to work—every routine activity becomes an altar upon which we leave our small offerings of love. Prayer expands beyond mental thoughts or even stillness, becoming everything we do, every use of our "strength." When prayer involves head and heart, being and action, prayer becomes the present moment itself. Worship is not a separate activity but is embedded within all activities conducted for the love of God. Life becomes one, a united experience.

You no longer live a dual life of spiritual apartheid, moving toward "godly" activities or "Spirit-filled" places as an antidote for the barrenness of your secular living. Brother Lawrence says that "our sanctification did not depend upon *changing* our works, but in doing that for God's sake which we commonly do for our own."[14] It's not necessary to take more missions trips or attend more church services to awaken us to Christ's presence in our lives. We simply practice God's presence within all our activities, open ourselves to the Lord in all times and places. The line between secular and sacred slowly erases, and we realize the true self has emerged into the smallest corners of our living. Practicing the Presence is about living life as an ever-unfolding love affair with God. And isn't this what you've wanted all along? You experience eternal life—your tender union with Jesus—both in your disciplines and in how you move through your day. Colossians 3:11 becomes the culmination of your living: "Christ is all, and is in all."

Sacred Living Here and Now

Simple awareness of life, awareness of God, and practicing God's presence are disciplines that open eternity to temporal humanity. But perhaps such a life sounds like traversing up the mount and encountering a transfigured Jesus; all you need do is build your shelter and order iced tea. All this talk sounds idyllic. We might desire to stay perfectly in the Presence, fully awake to life with undivided attention on eternity. But this is not the whole of reality. And maybe you're afraid it's all or nothing, and returning to the valley signals that Jesus' unveiled glory must fold itself away into some drawer, buried from the daily.

I'm fatigued as I type these words. I was up in the night worried and praying for a friend who's making potentially devastating life choices. I'm concerned about completing the manuscript for this book on time; it's slower and more arduous than I'd anticipated. In addition, the new owner of my apartment building is raising the rents sky-high, so I need to find another place to live. I sometimes find myself, instead of practicing God's presence, practicing the presence of people and situations that perplex and trouble me. You, too, have your own troubles and concerns, your personal sorrows and sadness. Perhaps the moments you spend reading this book before bedtime or on the bus are the only quiet space in your day. Perhaps you experience frightening absences that haunt the edge of your existence even while you wish to be devoted to the Lord.

Sometimes, practicing God's presence feels alien and impossible as if I'm in a mud slide, grappling for a handhold. I'm sure it's the same for both of us. In light of how life really goes, is it possible, is it practical, to really live the intentional life? With all of my fragile, fractured being, I must say "yes." And so must you.

Practicing the presence of God, first of all, takes practice. As a true-self-emerging person, don't measure or seek perfection that puts the focus back on yourself. Instead, be amazed and encouraged by the one hour or so that you might have dwelt in God's presence, rather than despair over the fourteen you spent elsewhere. As you practice God's presence, your image of God will become healed and your true self will emerge. The superficial facade of the false self will flake away. In time, practicing the Presence opens you to a re-created life, to the holiness of the ordinary, which is, in truth, never again ordinary. Everyday living slowly becomes sacred ground, the place of unending eternal encounter. The intentional life, while a bit muddier than you might have hoped, is within reach. It is living life as a sacred gift, receiving each moment as a precious treasure. More and more you understand that God's goodness is declared everywhere you look.

The bushes are burning all around us, even in that which we call mundane. Frederick Buechner gives one of the best summaries of the intentional life that I've ever encountered: "There is no event so commonplace but that God is present within it, always hiddenly, always leaving you room to recognize him or not to recognize him, but all the most fascinatingly because of that, all the more compellingly and hauntingly. . . . Listen to your life. See it for the fathomless mystery that it is. In the boredom and pain of it no less than in the excitement and gladness: touch, taste, smell your way to the holy and hidden heart of it because in the last analysis all moments are key moments, and life itself is grace."[15]

To nourish such a life, we must learn, as Buechner advises, to listen to our lives, which means to listen to the right voices. Many voices bid for our attention hour by hour. Most of them are false-self voices, either from within or without, compelling us toward choices shaped by drives for security, esteem, and power. And all of us have said "yes" to such voices at different times, and some of us have lived our whole lives enslaved by such voices even while proclaiming Christ.

Practicing God's presence is the culmination of intentional living and creates a prayerful existence that empowers you to stand at the crossroads and choose God. During one of Jesus' temptations in the wilderness, he responds to Satan, "Man does not live on bread alone" (Matt. 4:4). And in our culture the same tempter tells us that all we need is bread. We're pushed to chase after whatever looks breadlike, to satisfy our more petty and superficial appetites. But as you grow to love Jesus more fiercely, you can choose a life that hinges "on every word that comes from the mouth of God."[16]

And when your life depends upon every word that God speaks, when you dwell within the Lord's presence, intentional living then becomes a life of vocation. *Vocation* in its Latin root means *to call* and is God's call upon the whole of our lives. As a true-self-emerging person, your activities are not merely busy-ness, your job not just work, your ministry not only things you perform for God. The voices of the old self are slowly replaced, not with another set of activities but with vocation, God's call upon you.

But how do you hear the voice of God in your search for vocation? Once when I was laid off from a job and feeling greatly depressed and lost, I signed up for a job seekers seminar at my church. There, a chipper Christian job coach exhorted us to find work that was vocation, that made us happy, indicating that it was God's desire that we find fulfilling work. I had just left employment that felt dry, barren, and distinctly *un*happy. I felt stunned that God would care that I enjoyed my work and that enjoyment was an indicator of vocation. Too often we re-spond to the voice of the "oughts" or to the old self's drive for security. But if we live in the presence of God, we can more and more trust the passions that God has breathed into us, moving toward the gladness that God gives us. Frederick Buechner says:

> Maybe . . . the voice we should listen to most as we choose a vocation is the voice that we might think we should listen to least, and that is the voice of our own gladness. What can we do that makes us gladdest, what can we do that leaves us with the strongest sense of sailing true north and of peace, which is much of what gladness is? . . . I believe that if it is a thing that makes us truly glad, then it is a good thing and it is our thing and it is the calling voice that we were made to answer with our lives.[17]

Buechner, elsewhere, expresses his idea of vocation more succinctly: "the place where your deep gladness and the world's deep hunger meet."[18] Perhaps this sounds at odds with your spirituality, which too often says, "If I don't want to do it, then it's probably God's will that I do it." Thus, if your greatest fear is being a missionary in Africa, then you can be sure that's where God will call you to go. This is the voice of the false self, who must tiptoe around a mildly cruel and unsafe God. We have done violence to ourselves with such notions.

When I look at the world, the Christian community included, I see a deep hunger. And maybe the most necessary thing, maybe the *only* thing, that can genuinely feed this world's hunger is for women and men, fully alive in God, to actualize a life of gladness. Perhaps the kind of life where the kingdom of God can flow unimpeded is in works that are fueled by passions that embody the thrill of relationship with God and that are congruent with how God designed us.

Whenever I counsel students on college majors and life direction, I never ask them what they're good at or which of their skills are most marketable. I ask them what their passions are. I tell them to give those passions to God while seeking him, without a huge concern about future employment. I'm aware that mine is often the lone voice in the wilderness, and I wonder where these young ones will be in twenty years if at nineteen they're stuffed into straitjackets of the sensible. I fear that the messages we send will have them waking up at forty or fifty, wondering where their lives went. And they will realize how much their faith has acquiesced to the culture. They'll understand they're living someone else's idea of their lives. Some of you are there right now.

When I was in my early thirties, out of work, scared, and struggling with vocation, someone gave to me a great piece of advice: Move your life in the direction of your dreams, not in the direction of your fears. Many people say they believe in an Almighty God but direct their lives as if God could fit in a matchbox. If we, as Christians, cannot plunge off the map of this culture's wisdom, then what hope is there for anyone else? True, vocation carries with it its own sacrifice, but the greatest and saddest sacrifice is to function within a life that's not really yours. And I believe God will make room for your passions if you will but fling yourself upon his character. No other response is big enough for the God we serve. Naive? Of course, but our congregations are pallid for lack of this kind of naiveté. This is why Paul must remind us, "No eye has seen, no ear has heard, no mind has conceived what God has prepared for those who love him" (1 Cor. 2:9).

Perhaps such a call to gladness sounds too self-indulgent or even—shall I say it?—too enjoyable. But only a kingdom made up of passionate, God-enthralled people will ever make the Good News look like good news. The Westminister Catechism declares that the chief aim of man is to glorify God and enjoy him forever, echoing Scriptures such as Psalm 37:4: "Delight yourself in the LORD and he will give you the desires of your heart."

The Prayer of Examen

In Psalm 26 David says, "Test me, O LORD, and try me, examine my heart and my mind" (v. 2), and in Psalm 139, "Search me, O God, and know my heart; test me and know my anxious thoughts. See if there is any offensive way in me, and lead me in the way everlasting" (vv. 23–24). The practice of godly examination is part of intentional living. Ignatius, a spiritual writer and leader who lived in the early 1500s, recommended to his community that they participate regularly in a prayer of examen as part of their growth in holiness and sanctification. As the word indicates, a prayer of examen encourages us to examine our lives, not in the way of dissecting our every move on a petri dish—which is self-absorbed—but in the way of careful noticing. Ignatius spoke of locating, day by day, our moments of consolation and desolation, and by identifying such moments, we come to understand God's will.

The authors of the book, *Sleeping with Bread,* have translated Ignatius's examen into a more tangible and contemporary format that even small children can enter into. They suggest that at the close of each day, a candle be lit, symbolizing God's presence, and after allowing a few minutes of silent reflection, two questions be prayerfully asked: "For what moment today am I most grateful? For what moment today am I least grateful?" They give other ways to ask these two questions: "When did I give and receive the most love today? When did I give and receive the least love today. When did I feel most alive today? When did I most feel life draining out of me? What was today's high point? What was today's low point?"[19] After identifying these moments, the time is closed with prayer, thanking God for all the day's moments.

The examen can be done alone or with another. Parents can guide their families through the examen at mealtime or when tucking little ones into bed at night. This prayer helps us to stay present to our lives and to where we consciously experience God in our day. The two gratitude questions enable us to locate the moments of our day when we were present to God and giving or receiving his love (our consolations) and to locate moments when we cut ourselves off from his presence, refusing to give or receive God's love (our desolations). This prayer can be done mentally, verbally, or in written form. I have, at times, kept a notebook in my nightstand for the examen. In a few sentences, I journal my most and least grateful moments, including a list of five or more things for which I was grateful during that day. The process takes only a few minutes, and, says Merton, nurturing gratitude re-creates the goodness of God within us, helping us "to recognize the Love of God in everything he has given us—and he has given us everything."[20]

The examen can help you discern God's voice as he refines your journey in both small and large ways. Being late or overly rushed for an appointment was, for instance, often my least grateful moment. From that I learned to leave early in order to arrive at my destination relatively centered. My most grateful moment often surrounded weekly corporate worship. In response I've cultivated new spaces for personal worship. On a larger scale, I've realized that many of my most grateful moments surround writing projects, such as this one, so I believe part of my life's vocation, God's call upon me, is spiritual writing.

While the prayer of examen assumes that our lives contain a holy purpose, it also recognizes that our culture distracts us from that purpose. Destiny will not simply be dropped upon our heads (Paul's Damascus road experience aside). We must welcome it in godly watchfulness. Whether or not this specific prayer is used, the point is to be aware of what is happening around and within us, recognizing consolations and desolations, thus seeking God in all our moments.

Too much of living is spent robotically moving from one event to another, estranged from our personal history and bewildered as to where God is in our journeys. We all desire direction, but we don't always live the kind of life that can prepare us to make critical decisions. And when such decisions are needed, we are suddenly interested in a crash course on intentional living; we ask, "Should I leave my job?" or "Should I start a new ministry?" and attempt discernment around such questions. Good enough, but if you've lived an intentional life, guidance arises more naturally because you live in awareness of God, of yourself, and of the spiritual content of your days. You've identified your consolations on a regular basis and can more easily recognize your passions, making God-ward changes to ultimately live more and more in the love of God and his will for you.

Living Fully, Living Well

William Stafford begins a poem that involves self-examination, "Some time when the river is ice ask me mistakes I have made. Ask me if whether what I have done is my life."[21] It's a haunting question: Is what I'm doing *my* life, the life God intends for me? Is what you're doing *your* life? Are you involved in work, in relationships, and in a daily way of being in the world that is not *your* life, not your gladness, not your vocational call? Many of us are. And why? Maybe we're afraid—afraid to risk, to forsake our safe existence cushioned by security, esteem, and power. And more—afraid of passion, of opening our dreams and desires to the all-consuming heart of God. If so, then what we fear is living itself. C. S. Lewis brilliantly sums up our situation:

> Indeed, if we consider the unblushing promises of reward and the staggering nature of the rewards promised in the Gospels, it would seem that Our Lord finds our desires not too strong, but too weak. We are half-hearted creatures, fooling about with drink and sex and ambition when infinite joy is offered us, like an ignorant child who wants to go on making mud pies in a slum because he cannot imagine what is meant by the offer of a holiday at sea. We are far too easily pleased.[22]

I have no interest in living a manageable life. I don't want the life I am capable of conjuring and sustaining. Sometimes I lose my way, give in to fear, but I intend my living to be a godly adventure. Too many settle for halfhearted pursuits, a passionless existence, the dress rehearsal.

Intentional living is daily, moment by moment, decision by decision. It's also opening up life to a wide-angle lens. *Sleeping with Bread* suggests that we do what the authors call a final examen. They tell the story of Sam, a man who had lived unintentionally, lost in busyness and in an existence that was not really his. Sam went on a retreat where the leader led the group through a final examen prayer: "In your prayer imagine that you are seventy-five years old and dying. See the events of your life flash before you. For what are you grateful? What do you wish you had done differently? Pay special attention to the years between your present age and your death." The final examen changed Sam's direction: "After that exercise of a final examen of my life, I knew I didn't want to die in front of a computer screen. I wished I had spent the remainder of my life counseling alcoholics and broken families. So I quit my computer job and began taking college classes to get a counseling degree. Meanwhile I've been working as a lay counselor with alcoholics. Since that decision I enjoy life, and I feel at peace that I'm doing what I was sent here to do."[23]

Can you prayerfully picture yourself at seventy-five (or ninety-five if you're already older, or forty-five if you're a very young adult)? For what would you like to be most grateful for having done with your life? What do you believe you'd be least grateful for? Let your answers open up a dialogue with your Beloved, the God who intends for you to live with outrageous fullness.

The intentional life is within your reach. You can venture into vocation, a wakefulness, that allows the dreams God has for you to take on flesh in your living. Return to the verses from Ephesians 5. Read them slowly, listen to them carefully. As they soak into your heart and mind, pause after each line and ask, "God, what do you want to say to me through these words?"

> For you were once darkness,
> but now you are light in the Lord.
> Live as children of light. . . .
> This is why it is said:
>   "Wake up, O sleeper,
>   rise from the dead,
>   and Christ will shine on you."
> Be very careful, then, how you live—
> not as unwise but as wise, making the most of every
>   opportunity,
> because the days are evil. . . .
> Speak to one another with psalms, hymns and spiritual songs.
> Sing and make music in your heart to the Lord,
> always giving thanks to God the Father for everything,
> in the name of our Lord Jesus Christ.

These words are not just good ideas to be highlighted in yellow during our devotions. We can do more than that with them. They are a call to be answered, as God shepherds our days. And so we must choose.

Deuteronomy 30 urges us to choose life, to choose God, as

we cross the Jordan of our lives into new and uncertain lands: "I have set before you life and death, blessings and curses. Now choose life, so that you and your children may live and that you may love the Lord your God, listen to his voice, and hold fast to him. For the Lord is your life" (vv. 19–20). The Lord himself is my life, your life. All else is shadow. May you with him, in him, through him shape an intentional life where his love claims you more completely, where his wild, expansive call to you is answered with your whole being—heart, soul, and mind. This is our destiny and our privilege. There is none greater.

9

THE TRUE SELF IN COMMUNITY

Learning to See

By this all men will know that you are my disciples,
if you love one another.

—*Jesus (John 13:35)*

So very often, many outpourings of affection for God, of resting
in God's presence, of good feelings towards everyone and
sentiments and prayers like these, although very good and very
desirable, are nonetheless suspect if they do not express themselves
in practical love which has real effects.

—*St. Vincent de Paul*

Now that you know these things, you will be blessed if
you do them.

—*Jesus (John 13:17)*

It was the first night of the conference, and the speaker was little known to our church. Despite our promises as organizers, we had barely broken even on the expenses for the event. But

that first night, Brennan Manning—now a readily recognizable
name in many evangelical circles—stood before about a hundred of us and posed a question and response that I will never
forget. "Who's the most Christlike person in this room right
now?" An uneasy silence ensued as he allowed us to ponder his
question. He continued, "It's not the person who prayed the
most or the person who read his or her Bible the longest or
even the person who did the most acts of service today. No, the
most Christlike person in this room right now is the person
who is the most choked with compassion over the brokenness
of his or her neighbor. Because we are never more like Christ
than when we are overcome with love and compassion over the
poverty of our neighbor."

Brennan's words are not only profoundly true, they cut
through the clutter of what we as Christians say versus what we
do. We all agree with the clever credo, "The main thing is to
keep the main thing the main thing." But when it actually comes
to doing the main thing—loving others—there's a huge discrep-
ancy between words and actions, between thought and behavior. Like the Pharisees, we might applaud compassion in
principle but reject it in our actual living.

Bible verses extolling the love of God, proclaiming love as
his essence, and compelling us to compassion are the cornerstone of our faith. John says it simply: "God is love. Whoever
lives in love lives in God, and God in him" (1 John 4:16); "As
you have heard from the beginning, his command is that you
walk in love" (2 John 1:6); and "Dear children, let us not love
with words or tongue but with actions and in truth" (1 John
3:18). And Jesus sums up everything: "Love the Lord your God
with all your heart and with all your soul and with all your
mind and with all your strength. . . . Love your neighbor as
yourself" (Mark 12:30–31). Jesus beckons us to plunge into a
life where the love of God claims us completely, where every
thought, every action, and everything we're about is a unified
response of love to God and humanity. The magnitude of this
call is staggering. It should awaken and inspire and electrify

every fiber of our beings. It is an unequivocal call that should utterly consume and devastate us in its immensity.

But the command to love has become cliche, rarely moving us anymore. Our response is flattened by an abstract faith that is more interested in power than in the impoverished, that is more energized in being right than in being righteous, that is more desirous for comfort than for compassion. Day after day, legalism and condemnation are chosen over love and grace with catastrophic results: "The number of people who have fled the church because it is too patient or too compassionate is negligible; the number who have fled because they find it too unforgiving is tragic."[1] Debates over new buildings, church finances, and who wields power generate more heat than how to fulfill the commandment to love. As weak and wounded people, we, of course, stumble in our endeavors to love others. But the failure to love goes beyond attempting to fulfill a vision and falling short. Rather, there is little vision to aim at and too few attempts to hit the mark—making the love of God truly define our presence in the world. When we honestly look at our lives, we must admit that we are simply more interested in using our attention, time, and energies for other things.

In evangelical circles, we focus on accurately dividing the Word of Truth—and rightfully so. But in guarding our pure and undiluted theology, heresy has slipped in the back door. We have become functional heretics, disbelieving with our actions what we say is true in our theology—the absolute primacy of loving others as the central mark of our Christian faith. But it's not enough to simply have a cognitive belief in love's centrality.

In reality, while we say compassion is essential, we behave as if it is optional. On the other side of the coin, when we demonstrate compassion, it is often spurred by something other than the love of God. The false self may act compassionate to satisfy its drive for esteem or to fortify its sense of power and control. Or the motivation is extrinsic, a response to "shoulds" or communal expectations. And many might quote James 2: "As the

body without the spirit is dead, so faith without deeds is dead"
(v. 26). But we must turn this verse around, recognizing that
deeds apart from a love inspired faith are equally dead.

There exists, too, a type of counterfeit true self that is im-
mature and self-indulgent. Such believers seem to experience
the love of God and speak at length of ecstasies with the Lord.
But their experiences of God's love rarely move these people
outside of themselves and into practical demonstrations of
compassion. And when it does, their acts tend to be highly
visible.

Although our problems and pitfalls in regard to compassion
are many, compassionate presence is still the one mark of people
who belong to Jesus. And the point of our contemplative disciplines, our intentional living, our practice of God's presence
culminates in compassion. If we really are true-self-emerging
people, the fruit in our daily living enlarges the reality of God's
kingdom for everyone we encounter. This movement towards
others in genuine, Christ-filled compassion is the ultimate sign
of the presence of the true self.

Churches tend to talk about compassionate service only in
terms of measurable behavior. The vision and the self we bring
to such service is considered secondary if at all. As the previous chapter pointed out, living intentionally requires us to see
reality as it truly is. To be a compassionate presence, we must
view our neighbors through a different lens. We must see others the way Jesus does.

Christ in the Other

This final chapter will not give strategies for ministry or contain exhortations on the need to engage in selfless service.
Many others have well articulated such subjects. I only claim
that such actions need a complement. In the area of compassionate presence and service we need transforming vision, not
merely a set of behaviors. Because when we are transformed,
we begin to see differently, and then strategies for service and

ministry have meaning and fullness. Compassion begins not with actions but with a way of seeing that stimulates a passionate and tangible response. The following story illustrates how the most powerful and durable compassion is ignited through godly vision.[2]

A gifted and loving rabbi, young in years, was entrusted to direct a seminary that trained men to become rabbis. Such an opportunity had been his dream, so the rabbi watched with delight as the men arrived, and the men themselves were filled with joy and wonder at this new venture. Greetings and blessings spilled across the dining hall, and much laughter erupted as they went about their assigned chores. They studied the Torah together, the quicker students helping the less adept. A lively camaraderie was forged in a short span of time.

But as routine set in and the stress mounted, the community's life began to crack. The students studied together less often, trying instead to outdo each other with their answers in class. They began to resent their assigned chores, grumbling and performing them with resignation. Backbiting and gossip became the norm. Perplexed and distressed, the young rabbi delivered long sermons on Yahweh's love and call to obedience and daily admonished individual students to love their brothers. Things would change for a day or two. But the scornful behavior always returned.

One day as the rabbi walked into town, he encountered one of his mentors from his own seminary days, now a wise and venerable old man. The younger rabbi quickly poured out his frustration and sorrow to the elder, begging him to help. The old man listened and agreed to visit the community. "I'll come," he said, with a shrug of his shoulders, "and I'll do what I can."

A few days later, the older rabbi arrived. The younger one waited for his former mentor to gather the men and deliver one of his fiery speeches that would surely revive their hearts. Or perhaps he would send the students out to minister to the poor and then brotherhood would resurrect. Or maybe he would assign them a text on how to live the life of love, and the words would heal their hate. Nothing like this happened. The elder quietly moved among the seminarians during his two-day visit, taking aside a student here and there, having a short, whispered conversation with each.

The young rabbi was enormously disappointed, convinced his mentor had failed him. But over the course of several days, he noticed changes, small at first, within the students. They began to cluster more in study groups, eagerly sharing their insights. Gladness characterized their communal work duties. And mealtimes were sometimes slowed because each one insisted that the other be served first. A new reverence and compassion consumed the community, displayed in both word and action. The rabbi was astounded and overjoyed at the wondrous metamorphosis. The community was loving, vibrant, more so even than in the beginning.

Several months later, the rabbi again encountered his mentor. He regaled his old friend on the tremendous changes that followed his visit, marveling at the transformation. "Tell me what you did," he implored. The elder breathed deeply, smiled, and replied, "I simply spoke to each young man and said to him, 'I have something to tell you that you must keep secret from the others. It is breathtaking news, so listen carefully. It has been revealed to me that one of the young men in your community is the Messiah.'"

Image Bearers of God

In this story, external pressures to create compassionate community were insufficient in the face of innate human sinfulness. What created deep change was how the students saw each other. They were transformed when they considered that the young man next to them might be the Messiah.

The rabbis were waiting for the Messiah to come; but for us he has already come and makes his home within each member of the Christian community. And beyond—the image of God is lovingly imprinted upon every human soul. The triune God said, "Let us make man in our image, in our likeness, and . . . so God created man in his own image" (Gen. 1:26–27). Whether or not we acknowledge it, every human being walking the earth at this moment is created in God's image, and the vitality of the Christian community hinges upon the degree to which we see and experience Christ in the other.

Jesus doesn't encourage us to merely *treat* others as if they were Christ himself but, deeper, to actually *see* the other as Christ: "Whatever you did for one of the least of these brothers of mine, you did for me" (Matt. 25:40). Something of God resides in the other. The more we experience others in the awareness of Christ's splendor encased in clay, the more loving service becomes a natural response. The glory of God is within us, where the risen Christ, in the words of Merton, sleeps like dynamite in our paper flesh. The friend you have cappuccino with, the woman at the desk next to yours, the man who cut you off on the highway—all bear the image of God as actual or possible members of Christ's holy body.

And if I see all as image bearers of God, my compassion must be lavishly consistent. We tend to pick and choose who is worthy of our compassion and who isn't. If my compassion for a two-year-old child suffering from cancer is any less than for the drunk driver who crashed into a tree and now lies mangled in a hospital bed, then I am not loving with the love of God. I am called to not discriminate, to not use my energy weeding out applicants whom I deem undeserving of my love. In light of how Jesus cried out to his Father to forgive his torturers, my love for others must be equally outrageous and undeserved.

Anthony DeMello offers helpful images to understand this kind of compassion:

> Take a look at a rose. Is it possible for the rose to say, "I'll offer my fragrance to good people and withhold it from bad people?" Or can you imagine a lamp that withholds its rays from a wicked person who seeks to walk in its light? It could do that only by ceasing to be a

lamp. And observe how helplessly and indiscriminately a tree gives its shade to everyone, good and bad, young and old, high and low; to animals and humans and every living creature—even to the one who seeks to cut it down. This is the first quality of compassion—its indiscriminate character.[3]

When I love with the compassion of Christ and not with a faint copy, judgments about worthiness are left behind. All people qualify for my love simply because they are human and, thus, image bearers of our wondrous God. To love in this way is to plow up all the hard ground present within my heart. Those of us who cling to the false self are powerless to love solely for the imprint of God's image. It is only within the liberty of the true self that we can hope to love indiscriminately: to love the unlovely, to love those who hurt us, to love even when it costs everything.

As with the seminarians in the story, in order to authentically love our neighbors as Christ, we must see our neighbors as Christ, not just theoretically but with true spiritual sight. And to become people with such lenses changes us. We will grow more Christlike. Thomas Kelly's poetic language describes what results from this transforming vision: "There is a tendering of the soul toward *everything* in creation, from the sparrow's fall to the slave under the lash. The hard-lined face of a money-bitten financier is as deeply touching to the *tendered* soul as are the burned-out eyes of miners' children, remote and unseen victims of his so-called success. There is a sense in which, in this terrible tenderness, we become one with God and bear in our quivering souls the sins and burdens, the benightedness and the tragedy of the creatures of the whole world, and suffer in their suffering, and die in their death."[4] Within such solidarity with God and humanity is a vision of life that leads us to love's ultimate conclusion—a place where our compassion for others more resembles that of the crucified Christ.

Love, Emma, and the Meaning of Life

Like the men before the rabbi's visit, I, too, possessed a largely cognitive knowledge of love. I knew the Scriptures on loving God and loving my neighbor, but for most of my Christian life, my compassion had been mostly limited to special times or especially lovable people. As I began to practice the presence of God and follow a more contemplative path in my disciplines, I awakened to another way of community life. I hungered to know more profoundly what it meant to love and to live in the kingdom of God. And one summer, I came to understand that how I relate to others is the purpose of disciplines and of life itself.

As a teacher, I treasure the summer months as a time to change the pace of life, recharge, and catch up. At the start of one particular summer, a routine medical exam brought up a health concern, a problem that might turn out to be small and negligible or signal something more serious. I was young enough and healthy enough that such things were new territory for me. I went through a period of uncertainty, which provoked honest conversation with God. I took long walks and prayed, wondering at the meaning of my life. Was my life eternally significant? If I were to find out I only had a short time to live, what would I change? I needed a clearly defined vision of what a meaningful, God-honoring life really was. But I chafed against verses such as Matthew's "seek first his kingdom and his righteousness" because they felt too vague to me. I could narrow down kingdom life to Jesus' greatest commandment: "Love the Lord your God with all your heart and with all your soul and with all your mind and with all your strength. . . . Love your neighbor as yourself" (Mark 12:30–31). Still, even this call appeared too obscure for me. Enough time had already been wasted. Whether life was to be short or long, I wanted to live in the marrow of what mattered most to God. I persisted in prayer, unwilling to let go until God answered me.

During this season of personal searching, I was also serving as an altar team member, providing prayer support to people after one of my church's weekend services. Once while praying after an assigned service, I could see several people waiting for prayer and recognized one of them. Emma had participated in a large community group of which I was a member some years before. For no good reason, I had always secretly disliked Emma. I felt as though she didn't really belong in the group—she was awkward, quiet, socially unskilled, but she showed up for everything. While I had never shared my feelings with anyone, they were potent. I had scorned Emma, and there she stood a few feet away in need of the loving intercession I was supposed to offer. The ugliness of my sin hung on me like a stone. I stood there with my partner, finishing up a prayer time, hoping another team would be freed up when Emma reached the front of the line. No such luck.

Even as Emma approached us, the Holy Spirit's conviction sliced through me with surgical precision. She spilled her story: she had a life-threatening illness, surgery was required, and while survival seemed likely, she was scared. Despite cowering under a huge dose of godly guilt, I managed to be fairly present to her, but my every gesture felt hollow and phony. She didn't know anything was amiss, and the three of us prayed for her surgery and for God to comfort and to heal her. This experience alone was enough to break me, but after a few minutes, Emma returned with her elderly mother. The mother was extremely frightened for her daughter, and she requested additional prayer. A few more hot coals were neatly piled on my head as I confronted the fact that this woman I denigrated was someone's much-loved child. The encounter ended, and the conviction stuck with me. But with my own health concerns still on the front burner, it eventually receded from my consciousness.

A couple weeks later, I received a good report, and my medical problem was resolved. I was fine. While sitting in church just after this news, feeling blessed and relieved, I learned Emma had died after her surgery. The unfinished work God had with me surrounding Emma, compassion, and the meaning of life came flooding back. I felt as if a steamer trunk had just been dropped on my head. Here I was perfectly fine, and this beautiful woman I had repeatedly scorned had passed away.

God relentlessly pursued my sin; I brimmed with tears for days. Every person I had ever treated in an un-Christlike manner had been rolled into one person—Emma. I realized, profoundly, that how I treat people matters. I had known this—everyone, of course, *knows* this—but I *felt* the truth in my bones, and I had the memory of Emma's face to haunt me with the reality of my darkened heart. Emma never once reverberated with the love of Jesus while in my presence, never felt the compassion of Christ flowing from my being. And I understood that sometimes we don't get second chances, that sometimes life is a lot shorter than we think. A shift in my future behaviors and attitudes could never change how I treated her. It was too late.

So I was caught in my miserable self, owning my brokenness, sorry for my sin, and waiting on God. In light of life and death, the temporal and the eternal, my need to concretely know the meaning of my life in Christ intensified. I had to live differently. I had to see differently. The old answers weren't working anymore. And, finally, God spoke.

I was reading the book *Centering Prayer,* and in it Basil Pennington told an anecdote about a seminary professor who had a tremendous impact on both his school and his students. Many followed this man into his field of theological study, and he was much loved. At his retirement celebration, he was asked to what he attributed his great success as a professor. He didn't hesitate to give away his secret: "I saw the image of God in each of my students, and I worshiped."[5] When I read those words, it was as if the wings of angels fluttered near my face. *This is it,* I thought. I stopped reading and sat quietly, but I was exploding inside. I knew God had just answered my prayer from earlier in the summer.

To see the image of God in the other and to worship. Suddenly, the command to be compassionate, to love others as Christ, found a new depth and clarity. As good as it is to love with the love of God, I realized this was not the final place to which God beckoned. I was called to something deeper—to worship itself. To see the image of God in others and to worship him through engagement with others is the culmination of loving Jesus, the purpose of community, and the greatest meaning of earthly life. After everything else is burned away or cast aside as rubbish, what remains, what matters, is that my relationships become so saturated with love and honor for others, that I become so aware that others bear the image of God as his beloved, that to simply be with another person is an occasion for worshiping God.

When most of us think of worship, we tend to gravitate toward the Sunday morning church experience. We love to sing our praises to Christ, thanking him, adoring and giving glory to his holy name. And we stop there. Worship is an extremely privatized experience—just Jesus and me. This form of worship is highly valuable, but I no longer believe it is of highest value to God. Yes, we are called to worship, but Jesus' most pressing command to us was not that we sing praises to God. In fact, in the Gospels, he never touches upon this form of worship. Instead, Jesus expressed to the Father, "I have brought you glory on earth by completing the work you gave me to do" (John 17:4). Jesus glorified God by loving people and by dying on the cross for them. Jesus taught and modeled how to live a worshipful life, a life that gives glory to God through compassionate seeing fleshed out in active love. What Jesus commanded most urgently, again and again, is that we love God through loving people, the precious lambs he came to save.

Jesus said, "A new command I give you: Love one another. As I have loved you, so you must love one another" (John 13:34). Our call is to love as Jesus loved, which means to love others in the same way and in the same manner. His love for us is a function of his oneness with the Father. Loving others in the way of Jesus is birthed from our unity with Christ, and to love in this way we must broaden our ideas about worship. Within such unity, worship becomes the recognition of God's image inscribed on human souls, and loving him through loving them.

This kind of worship can be costly—it cost Jesus his earthly life. But responding to the divine dimension in humanity and to the holy state of others as the beloved of God leads to a worship with more potential to transform the world and ourselves than does our more narrowly defined times of worship. What matters most in life, what comes through as gold in the fires of eternity, is that we love others so beautifully, so intensely, so aware of Christ-in-me that our interactions with others become worship—our love for God funneled through the other and raised as a sweet savor to his throne.

For me, this epiphany was wedded to my flesh-and-blood experience with Emma. The person I refuse to love is someone's son, someone's daughter. That person I scorn is Christ. The one I pass by is Jesus. Similarly, *you* are not commanded to be nice or to love in a mere ethereal sense. The call to live within your true self and to Christlike compassion is ultimately a call to worship. And, as Emma's death pointed out to me, it is a most urgent call.

There's only one hope to love in this divine manner—allow God to remove the scales from our eyes so that we might see our neighbors the way he does: as holders of the divine image within their immortal soul. C. S. Lewis sums up the recognition of God's image engraved upon every human being:

> It is a serious thing to live in a society of possible gods and goddesses, to remember that the dullest and most uninteresting person you can talk to may one day be a creature which, if you saw it now, you would be strongly tempted to worship. . . . There are no *ordinary* people. You have never talked to a mere mortal. Nations, cultures, arts, civilisations—these are mortal, and their life is to ours as the life of a gnat. But it is immortals whom we joke with, work with, marry, snub, and exploit. . . . Next to the Blessed Sacrament itself, your neighbour is

the holiest object presented to your senses. If he is your
Christian neighbour, he is holy in almost the same way,
for in him also Christ *vere latitat*—the glorifier and the
glorified, Glory Himself, is truly hidden.[6]

This kind of love is eternal life and fuses together as one the
two components of the greatest commandment: love God, love
your neighbor. Worship, then, truly becomes a way of life, a
God-filled way of being with others in the world. And when we
worship in this way, we begin to recognize Jesus everywhere
and to worship him through our love for others. This way of
seeing is a gift from God, a gift offered to us even now if we
desire to receive it. And that, of course, is the central question—do you desire this? A polite, performance-based arrangement with a God held at arm's length might produce the right
behaviors, but it will never touch pure, worshipful compassion.

In such a life, the love of God will more completely claim
you, and you will be ruled by your thirst for Jesus, your Beloved, whom you will seek and see everywhere. But how might
you more practically enter into this life? Two key elements of
worshipful living are the discipline of mindful availability and
the call to become people who bless.

Worshipful Living and Mindful Availability

How often do you truly feel listened to? I have a friend whom
I like, but whenever we're together, his attention is rarely trained
on me. When we're in conversation, he seems easily drawn
away by the distractions around us, his eyes darting about so as
not to miss anything. As a result, our level of intimacy is only
so-so. I know other people who give me half of their attention,
who seem to be thinking about something else or plotting a
rejoinder while I'm talking. I've washed my dishes while someone on the phone line was pouring out her heart to me. Students visit my office, and in my busyness I attempt conversation
while digging through a file or checking my e-mail. "I know it

doesn't look like it, but I *am* listening to you," I say, but if I truly gave such ones my full attention, I wouldn't need a disclaimer. But I am brimming with other things—people and places, future and past—things I must attend to. So how do we enter into worshipful relating? The entry point is to practice the spiritual discipline of mindful availability.[7]

Mindful availability is more than just giving someone our full attention, although for many of us that's a major step. Rather, mindful availability is a compassionate way of being present to people, a godly posture where we meet others in a worshipful way, a way that recognizes them as the image bearers they are. Mindful availability is a focused openness to the other, born of our attentiveness to God's presence in the present moment. You welcome others into the loving, ego-less space God creates within you for true-self ministry. Simple as it sounds, your full, compassionate, worshipful attention is one of the greatest gifts you can ever offer. Mindful availability is a spiritual practice that enables us to see all of life as a sacrament.

Many who do ministry use the "service project" approach; they show up, do a good deed, shake hands, and leave. And the more ministry they can pack in, the better. This approach ignores deep human longings while implementing product-oriented or "sophisticated" forms of service. But the greatest human need is to have someone be truly present to us, to be Christ to us in both our joys and pains. We desire to be heard; we ache to be known. We need human presence that unfolds into mindful availability. And perhaps some of us need to slow down, to do less ministry even, in order to enter into the tender ministry that is a quality of the heart.

Thus, mindful availability, while a prerequisite for compassionate service centered in Jesus, is in itself a meaningful ministry. My friend Jan's first seminary internship was in the Alzheimer's unit at a local care center. My initial thought was, *How unfortunate. The point of internships is to gain skills in ministry.* To my surprise, however, Jan said how much she treasured the experience. She spoke of how those most seriously afflicted with dementia were her favorites. She realized that she couldn't do anything for them or with them, so she just sat, engaging with her assigned patients in what she described as spirit-to-spirit contact. Only their minds were stricken. These people possessed an entirely coherent, God-engraved humanity. Knowing this truth, Jan experienced noncognitive ministry, ministry at the level of being, ministry as prayerful recognition of the human soul. Jan did, indeed, gain much-needed ministry "skills." Although she didn't use the term, she was practicing mindful availability to the Alzheimer patients—in her presence, ministering God's presence to them.

Such availability is something Jesus consistently offered to others. Blind Bartemaeus screamed from the side of the road, and Jesus, on his way out of Jericho, stopped and beckoned him to come. Jesus' whole attention centered upon this disheveled beggar: "What do you want me to do for you?" The woman at the well, a local whore, was converted to faith certainly by what Jesus knew about her, but more, I think, by his loving, nonjudgmental presence with her during their midday conversation. Or when a group of children was brought to Jesus, he insisted on holding and blessing each one individually, much to the consternation of the disciples.

Notice that all these examples were seeming "interruptions" in Jesus' schedule. An old university professor said, "My whole life I have been complaining that my work was constantly interrupted, until I discovered that my interruptions were my work."[8] As a result of practicing the discipline of mindful availability, I sometimes don't get to my car quickly after school, a trip through the grocery store could be delayed, or my morning of writing might need to create space for a troubled caller. But things do manage to get done, and my heavenly business is, ultimately, fulfilled in my presence to others.

Anytime I sense myself becoming frustrated with people wanting my attention and thwarting my best laid plans, I try to relax, center myself, open to God, while offering my hospitable presence to the person before me. Mindful availability means I am simply present to the other with my heart opened wide. To truly take others into my heart, I must not make demands that they think my way, convert themselves to something, or fulfill me in some manner.

To be present in this way propels me to self-abandonment, to vulnerability. It requires me, in a sense, to die. First John tells us, "This is how we know what love is: Jesus Christ laid down his life for us. And we ought to lay down our lives for our brothers" (3:16). Perhaps, for us, laying down our lives for our brothers and sisters is about offering the self-emptying compassion that motivated Christ's sacrifice: "In order to be of service to others we have to die to them; that is, we have to give up measuring our meaning and value with the yardstick of others. To die to our neighbors means to stop judging them, to stop evaluating them, and thus to become free to be compassionate."[9] Compassionate availability means having no thoughts toward my neighbor save those that the mind of Christ would conjure. My nitpicky ideas, judgments, desires for control, and preoccupation with my own image management must wither amid the lavish love of Christ that I offer through my presence to others. Dying to my neighbor, then, heralds the arrival of the true self in community. And when this occurs, I have truly become Christ to the other.

It's easy enough to think about mindful availability with those I am close to or to whom I minister. But what about my enemies, those who seek to triumph over me in some way? Am I to be available to these? "If someone strikes you on the right cheek, turn to him the other also. And if someone wants to sue you and take your tunic, let him have your cloak as well. . . . I tell you: Love your enemies and pray for those who persecute you, that you may be sons of your Father in heaven" (Matt. 5:39–40, 44–45). Jesus commands that I be present to the enemy, to offer my cheek in vulnerable availability, and to give the one who would swindle me more than he or she attempted to extort.

My friend Brian had a powerful experience of availability to the enemy early in his ministry as an associate pastor. Brian began to regularly receive harsh critiques, anonymously sent, of his addresses to the congregation—everything from sermons to how he did announcements. He suspected that the author of the notes was Ed, a crusty old man with significant influence in the church. Eventually, Brian received a phone call from Ed, who requested a meeting to "share" something with him. Brian drove to Ed's house, calculating and prerehearsing his verbal moves and how he might get the upper hand to triumph over this misguided man.

But before he could walk into the house, the Spirit of God spoke to Brian, saying, "Love your enemy." This stopped him. "How?" he wondered. The answer came: "Listen carefully, be attentive, and come as present as you can." With Brian's verbal artillery left at the doorstep, the meeting began. Ed opened a file folder with Brian's name on it and reported to Brian the date, time, and content of every instance when Brian had ever offended him. Brian recalls, "It took everything within me to stay right there, to not move away, to stay present." But he did and when Ed finished, Brian was quiet a few moments, and then he simply said, "You have taken great pains to document all your concerns. And if you think I can agree with you on everything, I cannot. But I appreciate the fact that you have wanted to meet with me and that you are in some way concerned about who I am. If something else ever comes up again, please feel free to call me or to come to talk to me right away." With that, Ed became visibly flustered, and the meeting quickly ended.

Two months later, Ed called Brian to set up another meeting to again express his dissatisfaction with Brian's performance since their last meeting. Brian, again, obediently gave the man his full presence and stayed available. During Ed's rant, Brian noticed that he mentioned having a son. That admission surprised Brian because the man never spoke of having children, and they certainly never came to church. At that point in the conversation, something shifted for Brian: "There was this little shaft of light and suddenly in a way I hadn't seen before, I realized this man bore the image of God, and there was something at work underneath all of this." Brian pursued discussion about Ed's children, and Ed eventually opened up, revealing his deep sorrow and regret concerning his relationships with them. The conversation closed three hours later with Brian and Ed praying together. The relationship was never the same after that encounter. Brian never again received anonymous critiques. Instead, he rejoiced in reports of Ed's inner journey with God and his reconciliation with his children. Looking back on the transformation of Ed and the relationship, Brian says, "I know this would never have happened had I treated him as my enemy. I realize I really became present to God in him. It galvanized the relationship. I had to say, 'There is the image of God, and if I despise this person, I despise the image of God.'"

Staying available to hurtful people may not end as well as Brian's experience with Ed, and we must discern those times when God's directive is to break off engagement with certain people. But Brian's story demonstrates how God can work through our mindful availability, our compassionate presence, even with those who seek to tear us down. The image bearer as enemy comes in many disguises: the hard-driven boss, the deceitful spouse, the angry neighbor, the unkind stranger. While we hold people accountable for their sins, we can still give them our presence, our availability. To do so seems costly, but not to do so is the thing we can least afford. Availability means, then, that you are simply here, in the present moment, living in the light of God's love as your true self, indiscriminately available to all. In this way, love your enemies with both prayers and prayerful presence to them in the name of Christ.

Worshipful Living and a Blessing Community

If we take seriously the call to worship God through our encounters with those who bear his image, we will want to practice mindful availability. And the substance of such interactions in the community—the prime marker that we are true-self-emerging people with divine vision—will be embodied in our delight in compassionately blessing one another.

And we need to be aware of what it means to bless. When we bless people, we are not simply patting them on the back for a job well done or noting their fine work. This is simply praise. Praising has value, but praising is not the same as blessing. To bless people is to remind them through our words or actions of who they really are, to recognize they are created in the image of God, and to speak of what is eternally true about them. To bless is to connect others to God and to their true-self identities in Christ. Henri Nouwen adds, "To give a blessing is to affirm, to say 'yes' to a person's Belovedness. And more than that: to give a blessing creates the reality of which it speaks."[10] And isn't this what we hunger for? To not just be affirmed in our doing but to have our true selves, our being, our eternal identity, reinforced by a blessing community?

The transforming power of blessing in your life and the lives of those around you can be inestimable. In *Life of the Beloved,* Nouwen, who spent the last years of his life pastoring a community for developmentally disabled people in Toronto, tells a story of how he came to understand the depth of our human hunger for blessing:

> Not long ago, in my own community, I had a very personal experience of the power of a real blessing. Shortly before I started a prayer service in one of our houses, Janet, a handicapped member of our community, said to me: "Henri, can you give me a blessing?" I responded in a somewhat automatic way by tracing with my thumb the sign of the cross on her forehead. Instead of being grateful, however, she protested vehemently, "No, that doesn't work. I want a real blessing!" I suddenly became aware of the ritualistic quality of my response to her request and said, "Oh, I am sorry, . . . let me give you a real blessing when we are all together for the prayer service." She nodded with a smile, and I realized

that something special was required of me. After the service, when about thirty people were sitting in a circle on the floor, I said, "Janet has asked me for a special blessing. She feels that she needs that now." As I was saying this, I didn't know what Janet really wanted. But Janet didn't leave me in doubt for very long. As soon as I had said, "Janet has asked me for a special blessing," she stood up and walked toward me. I was wearing a long white robe with ample sleeves covering my hands as well as my arms. Spontaneously, Janet put her arms around me and put her head against my chest. Without thinking, I covered her with my sleeves so that she almost vanished in the folds of my robe. As we held each other, I said, "Janet, I want you to know that you are God's Beloved Daughter. You are precious in God's eyes. Your beautiful smile, your kindness to the people in your house and all the good things you do show what a beautiful human being you are. I know you feel a little low these days and that there is some sadness in your heart, but I want you to remember who you are: a very special person, deeply loved by God and all the people who are here with you."

As I said these words, Janet raised her head and looked at me; and her broad smile showed me that she had really heard and received the blessing. When she returned to her place, Jane, another handicapped woman, raised her hand and said, "I want a blessing too." She stood up and, before I knew it, had put her face against my chest. After I had spoken words of blessing to her, many more of the handicapped people followed, expressing the same desire to be blessed. The most touching moment, however, came when one of the assistants, a twenty-four-year-old student, raised his hand and said, "What about me?" "Sure," I said. "Come." He came, and, as we stood before each other, I put my arms around him and said, "John, it is so good that you are here. You are God's Beloved son. Your presence is a joy for all of us. When things are hard and life is burdensome, always remember that you are loved with an everlasting love." As I spoke these words, he looked at me with tears in his eyes and then he said, "Thank you, thank you very much."[11]

Is this not what the community of God is intended to look like? Within this story, there is a sense of safety, of coming home, that is so rare and yet something every human being longs for at his or her center. I can't help but think that if this kind of blessing was typical in our faith communities, mobs of people would wait breathless for the church doors to open on Sunday morning. It is in such a community that Paul's prayer for the Ephesians could find flesh: "And I pray that you, being rooted and established in love, may have power, together with all the saints, to grasp how wide and long and high and deep is the love of Christ" (3:17–18).

When we do not bless others, we will curse them in some way. You might respond, "Well, I certainly don't curse anyone," but curses can be covertly tucked into many of our interactions. They can be layered into that which we identify as rather benign—our little criticisms, our small derisions. On the other hand, failure to bless others at a key moment can amount to a curse, that is, declining to affirm how God sees them. Sometimes a curse occurs simply because we have abdicated our spiritual call to bless. We think our blessings don't really matter, or we are uncomfortable delivering them.

Understand that we have no neutral encounters. Whether it's the pizza delivery guy or the person checking out our library books, we are called to bless all that bear the image of our Lord upon their immortal soul. If a kind word or a loving look can bless those with whom we come into momentary contact, how much more can we bless those in our immediate spheres of influence. Our families, our coworkers, our friends, even those whom we naturally dislike or do not get along with—

we must bless all, welcome all into the truth of how God sees them and what God says is true about them. Ignore the worldly lie that our blessing is unimportant or that not cursing is somehow sufficient. We either bless or we curse. People are a little better for having engaged with us or a little worse.

But in order to bless others, we must first "grasp" the blessing for ourselves. Many of us attempt to invite others into a spiritual reality that we ourselves are not experiencing. We desire to follow after God but were not blessed within our family systems or early faith circles. Because of this, we must place ourselves before the Lord in our spiritual disciplines and practice God's presence in our living. God eagerly desires to bless us, and his blessing will eventually drown out the curseful messages others have spoken over us. Psalm 115:12–13 says, "The LORD remembers us and will bless us: . . . he will bless those who fear the LORD—small and great alike," and the theme is also sounded in Romans: "The same Lord is Lord of all and richly blesses all who call on him" (10:12).

Blessing others is not a spiritual gift for a select few. Rather it is a natural outgrowth of grace for those who authentically experience God. The Lord himself gave this command to Moses, "Tell Aaron and his sons, 'This is how you are to bless the Israelites. Say to them: "The LORD bless you and keep you; the LORD make his face shine upon you and be gracious to you; the LORD turn his face toward you and give you peace." So they will put my name on the Israelites, and I will bless them'" (Num. 6:23–27). Blessing God's people was a priestly duty. Now, we, as the priesthood of believers, are called to demonstrate God's compassion through blessing others. When we are centered in the truth of our belovedness, our blessings will carry much spiritual weight. Amidst a world driven by scrambles for false-self power, there is one great, best use of the powers that God has entrusted to those who love him: the ability to bless.

Immersed in our own blessedness, we have the eyes of Christ to see the blessing of God that rests upon the other and to proclaim it with our words and actions. Blessing, as with compassion and availability, becomes not just an activity but a way of seeing and responding. And it is best not left to amateurs who would bless out of a sense of obligation or to demonstrate good Christian behavior. Blessing others is the business of sacredness, of touching what is sacred within the other with what is sacred within ourselves.

This is the community of Christ. We are God's blessed, beloved ones, enlarging the belovedness of another because we're so thoroughly showered with our own. Through blessing and being blessed, we more intimately experience God and our true selves. No other life path so thoroughly embodies the heart of God to the world.

Living a Salvational Life

It is rare, this living as a blessing community, marked by availability, this loving and cherishing each other in the name of Jesus. But while we can admit its rarity, we must also declare its normality. To not live in this manner is what's truly unusual. We must not view compassionate, worshipful living as the shining exception because, in truth, there is nothing special or spectacular about it. It is the Christian life Jesus modeled and the life he now empowers us to live. It is a life of love, at once holy and ordinary.

As Christians, love is the meaning of our lives, and our days are to be spent becoming more and more proficient at giving and receiving God's love. Compassion, worshiping God through mindful availability, blessing others in community—all these are fancy ways of talking about something so elementary yet something so central and profound: receiving the love of Christ, so we can give the love of Christ. Sometimes we try to make this truth of God more complex than it really is. But if at the end of our earthly existence, the sum of all we have done—our hymn singing, our Bible reading, our many prayers, our church work, our relationships, our thought life, even our very breathing— does not add up to being on a God-ward journey of becoming more loving, more honoring of others, and more compassionate, then we will have squandered the only earthly life we will ever be given. We will possess an existence trivialized by lesser pursuits, which contain little or no meaning in God's economy. One drop of cold water offered in love is more valuable than all the tomes written on the theology of compassion because within that single drop is the fullness of God. In view of God's great love and mercy, our energies best find fulfillment in loving others in the way we ourselves are loved by God. Any other life is unworthy of our call and of our identity as the beloved, true-self-emerging people of God. And the day we must begin is today.

How much longer do you plan to live on this earth? A few years? A few decades? Maybe another week? Many people who discover they have a terminal illness, who know their time is short, become more tender, more loving, and more open to God than they ever were when their earthly time felt endless. The fewness of days gives them a vision of what's truly important in life and the motivation to pursue it. We don't have to wait for our own death knell. We can live wisely and intentionally now.

In truth, we have only a hand span of days before us, and the time must be lived urgently. It's not too late to live the life that God has for you. We are called to be the hands, the feet, the very heart of our Lord Jesus, which was broken in reaching the world he died to save. And we are called to appropriate for ourselves, daily, moment by moment, his love that surpasses all knowledge. The call to salvation is now. God offers to you an eternal life, a true-self life, to be lived, beginning in this moment. This life is love itself, "the glorious riches of this mystery, which is Christ in you, the hope of glory" (Col. 1:27), and for some, this is a call to the salvation of your soul. For the rest, it is a call to the salvation of your days, a call to a salvational life immersed in Christ and his truth. His voice calls to you now as you stand at the threshold of all that remains of your time upon this earth. You are invited to live the glorious life of love you've been searching for all along.

Life is about starting over—again and again. It is a continuous realignment from faithlessness to faithfulness, the never-
ending return to the house of the Father, where we reaffirm
our "yes" to being the beloved. The time squandered can be
redeemed in the hands of our Lord. In light of the fierce love
of Christ and the emptiness of all that is not God, we can only
cry out with Peter, "Lord, to whom shall we go? You have the
words of eternal life. We believe and know that you are the
Holy One of God" (John 6:68–69). From across numerous gen-
erations of countless people who, with minuscule exceptions,
are now faceless and forgotten, Brother Lawrence speaks of
dedicating ourselves to the only reality that will outlast us:

> O Loving-Kindness so old and still so new, I have been
> too late of loving Thee. You are young, my brethren;
> profit therefore I beseech you from my confession, that
> I cared too little to employ my early years for God. Con-
> secrate all yours to His Love. If I had only known Him
> sooner, if I had only had some one to tell me then what
> I am telling you, I should not have so long delayed in
> loving Him. *Believe me, count as lost each day you have not
> used in loving God.* (italics added)[12]

Brothers and sisters, in the last analysis, there is nothing else
in this life but the love of God, no other meaning, no other
source, no other substance. This love is our heart's one call,
the destiny that transforms us into fire if we will only awaken to
it in this moment.

All I have left to offer is a prayer—for you and for me—that
we will continually awaken, continually give ourselves, wholly
and without reservation, to God. His wondrous love is who I
am, who you are, creating the precious gift of our true selves—
both now and for eternity.

ENDNOTES

Chapter 1: The Call to Communion

1. Thanks to the late evangelist Dave Busby for this metaphor.
2. Leanne Payne, *The Healing Presence* (Wheaton: Crossway, 1989), 84.
3. James Finley, *Merton's Palace of Nowhere* (Notre Dame, Ind.: Ave Maria Press, 1978), 122.
4. Ibid.
5. Thomas Merton, *Wisdom of the Desert* (New York: New Directions, 1960), 50.
6. Richard Foster, *Prayer* (New York: HarperCollins, 1992), 1.

Chapter 2: Discovering the Heart's Way

1. My ideas regarding the mind- and heart-centered approaches to God are loosely based on notes I took at a Pastoral Care Ministry conference in June 1995 led by Leanne Payne. She refers to the two postures as the *true* masculine and the *true* feminine.
2. Quoted in Madeleine L'Engle, *Walking on Water* (Wheaton: Shaw, 1980), 72.
3. Leanne Payne, *The Healing Presence* (Wheaton: Crossway, 1989), 139.
4. Ibid.
5. Oswald Chambers, *My Utmost for His Highest* (New York: Dodd, Mead, 1935), 42.
6. Kathleen Norris, *The Cloister Walk* (New York: Riverhead, 1996), 65.
7. Alan Jones, quoted in Payne, *The Healing Presence*, 119.
8. Payne, *The Healing Presence*, 119–20.
9. Leland Ryken, *The Liberated Imagination* (Wheaton: Shaw, 1989), 42–43.

235

10. Brennan Manning, *Abba's Child* (Colorado Springs: NavPress, 1994), 128.
11. Leanne Payne, *Listening Prayer* (Grand Rapids: Baker, 1994), 143.
12. Henri Nouwen, *The Way of the Heart* (New York: Ballantine, 1981), 78.
13. Thomas Merton, *New Seeds of Contemplation* (New York: New Directions, 1961), 183.

Chapter 3: Unmasking the False Self

1. James Finley, *Merton's Palace of Nowhere* (Notre Dame, Ind.: Ave Maria Press, 1978), 27–28.
2. Thomas Merton, *New Seeds of Contemplation* (New York: New Directions, 1961), 34–35.
3. Gerald May, *Addiction and Grace* (New York: HarperCollins, 1988), 98.
4. Thomas Keating introduces these drives in the book *Invitation to Love* (New York: Continuum, 1996).
5. Mother Teresa, *A Simple Path* (New York: Ballantine, 1995), xxii.
6. David Steindl-Rast, *Gratefulness: The Heart of Prayer* (New York: Paulist, 1984), 89.
7. Henri Nouwen, *Finding My Way Home* (New York: Crossroad, 2001), 30.

Chapter 4: Wounded Shadows

1. Thomas Merton, quoted in Basil Pennington, *True Self/False Self* (New York: Crossroad, 2000), 93–94.
2. Thomas Merton, *Contemplative Prayer* (New York: Image, 1990), 70.
3. Don Miguel Unamuno, quoted in Madeleine L'Engle, *Walking on Water* (Wheaton: Shaw, 1980), 32.
4. Jeanne Guyon, *Experiencing the Depths of Jesus Christ* (Sargent, Ga.: SeedSowers, 1975), 33.
5. Gerald May, *Will and Spirit* (New York: HarperCollins, 1982), 6.

Chapter 5: Ultimate Identity and True-Self Relating

1. Part of this image was inspired by a sermon by John Ortberg at Church of the Open Door, Minneapolis, Minnesota.
2. Thomas Merton, *Thoughts in Solitude* (New York: Farrar Straus & Giroux, 1989), 36.
3. Brennan Manning, *Abba's Child* (Colorado Springs: NavPress, 1994), 126.
4. Henri Nouwen, *Life of the Beloved* (New York: Crossroad, 1992), 39.
5. William Shannon, *Silence on Fire* (New York: Crossroad, 1991), 24–25.
6. Ibid., 25.
7. Ibid., 15. I have heard this story from various sources, but I first encountered it in *Silence on Fire*.
8. James Burtschaell, quoted in Brennan Manning, *Lion and Lamb* (Grand Rapids: Chosen, 1986), 19–20.

9. Ibid., 26.
10. Nouwen, *Life of the Beloved*, 90.
11. James Finley, *The Awakening Call* (Notre Dame, Ind.: Ave Maria Press, 1984), 71–72.
12. Jeanne Guyon, *Experiencing the Depths of Jesus Christ* (Sargent, Ga.: SeedSowers, 1975), 17.
13. Basil Pennington, *Centering Prayer* (New York: Image, 1980), 56.
14. Leanne Payne, *Restoring the Christian Soul Through Healing Prayer* (Wheaton: Crossway, 1991), 32.
15. Brennan Manning, *Stranger to Self Hatred* (Denville, N.J.: Dimension, 1982), 103.
16. Nouwen, *Life of the Beloved*, 106–7.
17. Ibid., 106.
18. C. S. Lewis, *Mere Christianity* (New York: Macmillan, 1952), 190.

Chapter 6: Blessing and Kingdom Living

1. Gerald May, *Addiction and Grace* (New York: HarperCollins, 1988), 42.
2. David Johnson, *Joy Comes in the Mourning* (Camp Hill, Pa.: Christian Publications, 1998), 18–20. This entire paragraph comes from this author.
3. Much of my thinking about the definition of brokenness comes from the work of David Johnson as given through teachings at Church of the Open Door, Maple Grove, Minnesota.
4. Henri Nouwen, Donald McNeill, and Douglas Morrison, *Compassion* (New York: Image, 1982), 19.
5. Henri Nouwen, *Can You Drink the Cup?* (Notre Dame, Ind.: Ave Maria Press, 1996), 33–34.
6. Henri Nouwen, *Life of the Beloved* (New York: Crossroad, 1992), 78.
7. Ibid., 79.
8. Percy Ainsworth, "Sin and Sorrow," *Weavings* 12, no. 6 (November–December 1997): 21.
9. Gerald May, *Will and Spirit* (New York: HarperCollins, 1982), 14.
10. Henri Nouwen, *Bread for the Journey* (New York: HarperCollins, 1997), January 2 entry.
11. Thomas Merton, *Thoughts in Solitude* (New York: Farrar Straus & Giroux, 1989), 36–37.
12. My reflections on this parable derive partly from a sermon by Jeff VanVonderan at Church of the Open Door, Maple Grove, Minnesota.
13. Johnson, *Joy Comes in the Mourning*, 21.
14. Sister Barbara Fiand quoted in Brennan Manning, *Abba's Child* (Colorado Springs: NavPress, 1994), 74.

Chapter 7: Disciplines of the True Self

1. Dallas Willard, *The Divine Conspiracy* (New York: HarperSanFrancisco, 1998), 36.
2. Dallas Willard, *Spirit of the Disciplines* (New York: HarperCollins, 1988), 156.
3. Richard Foster, *Celebration of Discipline* (New York: Harper & Row, 1978), 6.
4. Basil Pennington, *Centering Prayer* (New York: Image, 1980), 113.
5. These two principles are based on ideas presented in William Shannon's *Silence on Fire* (New York: Crossroad, 1991), but contain my own interpretation.
6. Larry Crabb, *The Safest Place on Earth* (Nashville: Word, 1999), 143, 146.
7. A. W. Tozer, *The Christian Book of Mystical Verse* (Camp Hill, Pa.: Christian Publications, 1991), vi.
8. William Johnston, ed., *The Cloud of Unknowing* (New York: Image, 1973), 54–55.
9. Henri Nouwen, *Here and Now* (New York: Crossroad, 1994), 72.
10. Ernst Kaseman, quoted in Brennan Manning, *Stranger to Self Hatred* (Denville, N.J.: Dimension, 1982), 36.
11. Pennington, *Centering Prayer*, 31–32.
12. Ibid., 32.
13. Macrina Wiederkehr, *A Tree Full of Angels* (New York: HarperCollins, 1988), 50.
14. Pennington, *Centering Prayer*, 72.
15. Many of my ideas about centering prayer are gleaned from the work of Keating and Pennington.
16. These thoughts by Keating came from a lecture he gave at the Centering Prayer Convention, St. Olaf Catholic Church in Minneapolis, Minnesota, 4 August 2001.
17. Pennington, *Centering Prayer*, 99.
18. Ibid., 97.
19. Ibid., 91–92.
20. Thelma Hall, *Too Deep for Words* (New York: Paulist, 1988), 2.
21. Henri Nouwen, *The Return of the Prodigal Son* (New York: Image, 1992), 43.
22. Johnston, *The Cloud of Unknowing*, 80.
23. Ibid., 60.

Chapter 8: Living the Intentional Life

1. Dallas Willard, *Spirit of the Disciplines* (New York: HarperCollins, 1988), 32.
2. William Shannon, *Silence on Fire* (New York: Crossroad, 1991), 31.
3. I believe legitimate outpourings of God's Spirit come with more intensity at certain gatherings at certain times. Such, however, are not the issue, nor do they excuse our embracing of spiritual apartheid.

4. These concepts are taken from Shannon, *Silence on Fire*, 73–74.

5. Richard Zenith, "Living the Eternal Moment," *Union Life* (July–August 1996): 5.

6. Jeanne Guyon, *Experiencing the Depths of Jesus Christ* (Sargent, Ga.: SeedSowers, 1975), 35.

7. This link between simple awareness and awareness of God is taken from Shannon, *Silence on Fire*.

8 Ibid., 38.

9. Ibid., 34–35.

10. Brother Lawrence, *The Practice of the Presence of God* (Grand Rapids: Spire, 1994), 20.

11. Ibid., 21, 26.

12. Leanne Payne, *The Healing Presence* (Wheaton: Crossway, 1989), 79.

13. Brother Lawrence, *The Practice of the Presence of God,* 17.

14. Ibid., 26.

15. Frederick Buechner, *Now and Then* (New York: HarperCollins, 1983), 87.

16. My thoughts in this paragraph on not living by bread alone have a loose base on Frederick Buechner's essay "The Calling of Voices," in *The Hungering Dark* (New York: HarperCollins, 1969).

17. Buechner, *The Hungering Dark*, 31–32.

18. Frederick Buechner, *Wishful Thinking: A Seeker's ABC* (San Francisco: HarperSanFrancisco, 1993), 119.

19. Dennis Linn, Sheila Fabricant Linn, and Matthew Linn, *Sleeping with Bread* (New York: Paulist, 1995), 6–7.

20. Thomas Merton, *Thoughts in Solitude* (New York: Farrar Straus & Giroux, 1989), 41–42.

21. William Stafford, "Ask Me," in *The Way It Is* (St. Paul: Graywolf, 1998), 56.

22. C. S. Lewis, *The Weight of Glory* (New York: Macmillan, 1980), 3–4.

23. Linn, Linn, and Linn, *Sleeping with Bread,* 12.

Chapter 9: The True Self in Community

1. Brennan Manning, *Abba's Child* (Colorado Springs: NavPress, 1994), 131.

2. I'm not sure whether I heard part of this story somewhere or whether I made it up. I have no clear memory of its origin. In any case, I've created its current form.

3. Anthony DeMello, quoted in Manning, *Abba's Child,* 76.

4. Thomas Kelly, *A Testament of Devotion* (New York: HarperSanFrancisco, 1992), 64.

5. Basil Pennington, *Centering Prayer* (New York: Image, 1980), 131.

6. C. S. Lewis, *The Weight of Glory* (New York: Macmillan, 1980), 18–19.

7. This term was coined by Sue Monk Kidd in an article, "Live Welcoming to All," *Weavings* (September–October 1997).

8. Henri Nouwen, *Reaching Out* (New York: Image, 1966), 52.

9. Henri Nouwen, *The Way of the Heart* (New York: Ballantine, 1981), 21.
10. Henri Nouwen, *Life of the Beloved* (New York: Crossroad, 1992), 56–57.
11. Ibid., 57–58.
12. Brother Lawrence, *The Practice of the Presence of God* (Grand Rapids: Spire, 1994), 111–12.